Your First Horse

Patrick Stephens Limited, part of Thorsons, a division of the Collins Publishing Group, has published authoritative, quality books for enthusiasts for more than twenty years. During that time the company has established a reputation as one of the world's leading publishers of books on aviation, maritime, military, model-making, motor cycling, motoring, motor racing, railway and railway modelling subjects. Readers or authors with suggestions for books they would like to see published are invited to write to: The Editorial Director, Patrick Stephens Limited, Thorsons Publishing Group, Wellingborough, Northants, NN8 2RQ.

YOUR FIRST HORSE
All the advice you need on buying, feeding and caring

by

Lesley Eccles
editor of *Your Horse* magazine

Patrick Stephens Limited

First published in 1990

Thanks to *Horse & Pony Magazine* for help with photographs, and to Carol Mailer of Beaconfield Equine Centre, Godmanchester, Huntingdon, for the use of facilities.

British Library Cataloguing in Publication Data

Eccles, Lesley
    Your first horse.
    1. Livestock: Horses. Care, — Manuals — For children
    I. Title
    636.1'083

    ISBN 1-85260-074-8

Patrick Stephens Limited is part of the Thorsons Publishing Group, Wellingborough, Northamptonshire NN8 2RQ, England.

Typeset by Harper Phototypesetters Limited, Northampton, England
Printed in Great Britain by Woolnough Bookbinding Limited, Irthlingborough, Northamptonshire

10 9 8 7 6 5 4 3 2 1

CONTENTS

INTRODUCTION

It is six am on a freezing December morning. A lone horse owner is on her way to care for her horse before going off to work herself. The ten-minute journey takes longer than usual because of the icy road conditions, but the young woman is still the first owner to arrive at the livery yard. Although the stable block is in darkness, she knows her own horse will be peering around the corner, looking for her and his breakfast! As her feet scrunch on the gravel, a low, welcoming whicker cuts through the frosty air — the woman snaps on the yard light and an expectant equine face is revealed, eyes blinking in the sudden brightness.

The woman talks to the horse, stroking his face and neck as she looks over the stable door to check for anything unusual in his stable. Uneaten food or heavily disturbed bedding would ring alarm bells in her head, indicating that all had not been well throughout the night. However, everything is all right and a smile brightens her face.

Still chatting to her horse, she empties his breakfast into the manger and sets about the tasks which make up the early morning routine. By the time she is ready for her homeward journey, the horse will have been thoroughly checked over, brushed and his feet picked out; stable rugs will have been swapped for outdoor rugs and the horse turned out for a spell in the field. She will have provided hay and checked the water supply in the field. The stable will have been mucked out and a bed laid down again, water buckets emptied, swilled out and refilled, haynet filled and tied ready in the stable with carrots left in the manger for the horse's return from the field. As someone else fetches in the horse whilst the owner is at work, the horse's stable rugs are left handy, along with the skip and hoofpick so the horse's feet can quickly be picked out.

Once all these tasks are completed the horse owner can return home and attend to her own needs. After work though, she still needs to see her horse — to feed, water and groom, to remove droppings and wet patches from his bed, and make it ready for the night, to adjust rugs and fill haynets, to keep her piece of the stable yard tidy and ensure that the horse's outdoor rug is dry and fit for use the next day.

In addition, of course, she has to fit in time for riding her horse; winter conditions often restrict safe riding to weekends only for working horse owners. There's still more to do — for instance hay, bedding and feed has to be bought, visits to the farrier have to be arranged every six weeks or so, while jobs like tidying the muck-heap and removing droppings from the field need to be done at weekends.

It is no wonder that the horse owner welcomes the longer days that spring heralds, bringing the chance of early morning rides before work or pleasant early evening hacks, the opportunity to compete at local shows, to attend riding club instructional sessions, explore bridleways with other horsey friends or simply let the stress of a working day disappear as horse and rider enjoy the scents and sounds of the countryside.

Having your own horse is a major responsibility, taking up amazing amounts of your time, money and energy. Yet it is also a most rewarding experience which will provide many superb moments of sheer pleasure, exhilaration, joy and a tremendous 'glad to be alive' feeling.

Extending your family to include a horse is not a decision to be taken lightly; once you have an animal, no matter whether it is a strapping horse or a tiny kitten, the welfare and life of that animal is in your hands. A horse will depend on you to provide him with everything, from food to exercise, water to first aid. You will have to learn to recognize signs of ill-health so that the horse receives any necessary treatment as quickly as possible. Through the bad times as well as the good days, a horse is dependent on its owner. It is not fair on any animal to deny him the everyday care he needs simply because the owner cannot be bothered, is tired, or finds the idea of shopping more attractive than riding out on a cold, wet day.

For many people owning a horse is a dream nurtured in childhood: the fulfilment of that ambition can be absolutely superb, but it brings with it a considerable price in terms of time and money. If you are interested in paying that price, then let's go deeper into the whole issue of having your own horse.

A HORSE OF YOUR OWN

Riding once or twice a week at the local riding school is one thing; having your own horse is another. For a start, there is always a horse for you to ride at your school, and even if your usual or favourite mount is off work through illness, there is generally plenty of choice for a replacement. But if your own horse is ill you're grounded, you have all the worry associated with a sick horse *and* you have the vet's bills to pay!

Of course, if you are late arriving for your lesson at a school someone will have tacked up the horse and have him ready and waiting for you. When it's your own horse no one is going to mollycoddle you — you will have to do everything yourself, unless of course, you can afford to pay someone else to look after the horse for you.

At a school, there is always someone to tell you what to do, give advice, lead the way on hacks. With your own horse the freedom to ride whenever you want means you also have to take the responsibility and the initiative, and ensure that your welfare, that of your horse and anyone you may ride with, is looked after.

No doubt you will have a favourite horse at your riding school, and no doubt he is a top choice with other people too. With your own horse there'll be no need to share a horse's loyalties with another person. As owner, provider of food, water, attention and lots of love, you'll be number one in your horse's life. Over the years you share together a bond will be built up, a relationship between you and your horse that no one can intrude on or take away from you. In the hectic world of today, it makes having your own horse worthwhile.

How will a horse affect my life?

The minute a horse enters your world you can guarantee that life will never be the same again. This is why:

Time This becomes a precious commodity. If you look after your horse yourself, then you are taking on a full-time, seven-days-a-week job which lasts for 52 weeks of the year and has no respect for holidays, Christmas, sickness or appalling weather. You will need to see your

Come rain, shine, hail or snow, looking after your own horse is a full-time year-round job.

horse at least twice a day, keeping to a routine — especially where feeding times are concerned.

If you are ill, then you have to make arrangements for someone else, who is also competent with horses, to care for your animal. Holiday plans also need to be organized carefully so that your horse is happy and safe whilst you're enjoying the sun and rest!

As a great deal of time will need to be devoted to the care and exercise of your horse, plus travel to him, to feed stores etc you need to organize other areas of your life as well. It is all a case of managing your time — but more of that later.

Money Whichever way you look at it, there is no cheap way to keep a horse. By sensible planning you can hold costs to a reasonable level, but keeping a horse properly demands a certain level of financial commitment over a long period of time. Think long and hard about the costs of horse ownership — it is not only the initial buying but also the constant upkeep which makes such a big hole in your monthly wage packet. Budgeting, which we'll look at soon, is an important part of your horse buying plan.

Home life A horse in the family will have repercussions on the other members of your household. For instance, other halves tend to object if they are always taking second place to the horse! You will need the support of your husband/wife/children/ boyfriend etc to ensure that the home fires are kept burning! The days of taking off for the weekend on a moment's notice will be gone — you'll have to think ahead and plan for your horse first. Visitors to your home for the weekend will have to realize that the horse still needs to be fed, exercised etc. All in all, you will have to become quite a resourceful diplomat if you are going to keep everyone happy most of the time!

Work life Horses thrive on routine so it is important to establish and stick to a routine which is sensible for you and your horse. If your job does not have regular hours then you need to organize a back-up team who can care for your horse in your absence. Horse owners who work flexitime or shifts often find it easier to ride in winter than other owners, but usually need helpers to step in at regular intervals during their working cycles.

If, after all that, you still feel that you really want a horse of your own, the next question is 'Are you ready for such a big step?' I have known of people who have had six riding lessons and then bought their own animal! On the other hand, there are people who ride and work with horses for years before making the big commitment of having their own.

One mistake you must not make is to think that once you have a horse you no longer need riding lessons. You can spend a lifetime with horses and still learn something new every day, so keep an open mind and continue to seek advice and help from others about your riding techniques and your general horse care.

Before buying your own horse you need to be a reasonably competent rider who can hack out safely and under control. A good way of increasing your skills and having an independent assessment of your abilities is to take the Association of British Riding Schools tests for weekly riders or the British Horse Society Horse Knowledge and Riding Stage examinations. These cover riding and stable management and include practical tests, providing you with a basic knowledge on which you can build. It is all good experience for the day your own horse arrives. Find out more from your local riding school or write to the two organizations concerned at the addresses listed at the back of this book.

Membership of your local riding club is also a boon as there is the chance of instruction and you will be mixing with other horse owners who will no doubt supply information and opinions.

There is also lots of sensible advice and help to be found in horsey publications such as *Horse & Pony Magazine* and *Your Horse*. The former is aimed particularly at younger owners, although many first-time horse owners of all ages look to its columns for help on riding, veterinary and stable management matters. *Your Horse* is primarily a horse care magazine, aimed at older people and carrying lots of useful features.

Every newcomer to horse ownership is bound to be a little daunted at the thought of coping with a horse, but the pressure can be eased by keeping your horse in a friendly yard where more experienced owners are available to help if problems arise.

Time management

Effective time management is something which everyone can learn and which can be applied to all aspects of our lives. All it involves is a little thought and planning.

Just think of the demands on your time — sleep, work (including travel to and from work), domestic responsibilities, eg cooking, washing, ironing etc, leisure time (eg with your horse, chatting to the neighbours, watching TV, family evenings out), personal time, eg bathing, washing your hair, visiting the hairdresser. An important aspect of time management is recognizing how much time you currently spend on your various activities and then evaluating the situation so you can become more effective. For example, you could save time by shopping once a month instead of every week. You could use lunch hours to pick up the fresh vegetables etc that you need weekly or pop into a farm shop on the way to your horse. On the horsey front, perhaps you could have a grand mucking out session at weekends and in the week skip out, replenishing bedding each day so the horse still has a clean comfy bed.

Think about all that you do. Is there a better way of doing everything? Is it vital to do everything? Could some things be left undone without harming anyone or anything? Can you ease the burden upon yourself? Delegation is another key to time management so why not ask other members of the family to load the washing machine/prepare the potatoes for supper etc?

Recognizing priorities is another vital ingredient to the effective use of time. For instance, at home you may be faced with several jobs which need attention, eg cooking the evening meal, ironing clothes for tomorrow, housework, washing the car. If you were really stuck for time then feeding the family would be first priority. Some jobs can wait until tomorrow, others cannot. Do first things first, and that applies whether it's your domestic life or your leisure time.

Make use of lists and then prioritize the tasks using an A, B, C system. Jobs labelled A must be done today, B jobs can wait until tomorrow if necessary, whereas C jobs can be delayed for several days. If you get through all your A tasks then you can start work on some of the B jobs or spend your extra time treating yourself to an extra long hack! If you do not manage to complete all your A jobs during the day then they must go to the top of the 'To Do' list for the next day.

Looking at this from a horsey standpoint, A tasks would be jobs like exercising and feeding, whereas tack cleaning could be a B priority and tidying the muck-heap/sorting out your tackroom could be classed as a C task. Mind you, it's important that you do get round to doing the C jobs eventually, otherwise you suddenly find that they've leapt up to an A category!

At all times tasks which affect your horse's daily welfare must have first priority. Your horse won't be too upset if the stable yard hasn't been meticulously swept every day, but he will be extremely bothered if he doesn't get his feed on time.

Another useful tip is to set yourself a time budget, eg, 15 minutes to vacuum the house throughout, 20 minutes to clean your tack. This helps you to be aware of time and concentrates your mind on the immediate task. Double up on work and leisure time where possible too, for instance by cleaning the tack whilst watching your favourite TV programme.

So remember, plan ahead and you will use time effectively. Make use of 'To Do' lists with prioritized tasks. Work to time budgets.

Preliminary budget

Assuming that you feel ready to take on a horse, let's get down to the realities of money and your horse budget. If horse ownership is your ambition, then you should have been saving hard! For many people it would not be wise to take out a loan in order to pay for a horse because the repayments coupled with the horse's upkeep could be crippling. Apart from the actual purchase price of the animal, there are other costs such as vetting, petrol costs (you could travel to see a dozen horses before you find a suitable one!), the cost of transporting the horse from his old to new home and so on. It is important, therefore, that you are prepared financially.

Keep your savings for a horse separate from other household money, and once you have a horse maintain your special horse account so that you can keep track of exactly how much your hobby costs you — something that will be invaluable when planning your horse budget for the next year. Whilst you do not have a horse, keep your cash where it will earn interest. Once you have a horse, if you can keep your account in credit a building society is a good place for your money. If the account sometimes operates in debit, then a bank account with an overdraft facility is worth negotiating. This will enable you to cope with unforeseen items of large expenditure, such as a huge vet's bill if your horse is sick for some time. Ideally, whatever type of account you have you need a contingency/emergency fund for any unexpected outlays.

Before you even start to look for a horse you need to know exactly what type of financial commitment you are taking on. Prices of horses vary according to their age, abilities, achievements, breed and height, so keep up to date with the market prices by scanning the 'Horses for sale' columns in your local newspapers and the equestrian magazines. As a first-time owner, a schoolmaster horse would be ideal, ie, one which knows its job and is sound, reliable on the road and in the stable, is easy to shoe, box, clip and catch. Naturally such paragons are in great demand and their asking price reflects this.

You will be able to get an idea of horse prices in your particular locality, but for the purposes of this exercise let us assume that to buy a 10-year-old, 16hh, half-bred horse we need to be thinking in the region of £1,500. But even if you have that much saved up, it is still too early to look for a horse. There are lots of other considerations.

Any prospective purchase will need to be vetted to ensure that it is in reasonable health and suitable for the activities you plan to undertake, eg, riding club events, hunting, dressage and so on. This cost is one you ignore at your peril. If the vet finds something wrong with the horse, such as a weak heart or a respiratory problem, he will tell you. Far better to have the disappointment before the horse is actually yours! There is more about vetting later, but for the moment add an extra £100 to your horse-buying budget! That is assuming that you only have one horse vetted — it is possible that your prospective horse will fail the vet, in which case you will be back to square one.

Once you've found a suitable horse and it has been given the all clear, you need to arrange transport home and insurance. It is possible to hire towing cars and trailers if you do not have your own transport or the seller may deliver the horse for a fee. Perhaps a friend with transport will help you out, but whatever arrangement you make allow a suitable sum in your budget.

Insurance cover is vital as soon as the animal becomes yours. Ask an insurance broker for advice on the various policies available and consult with other horse owners on their experiences of the various companies. (See **Stabled Horses** for more help on this subject.) If your horse is valued at £1,500 you should expect to pay £200 for a year's comprehensive cover and your premium will need to be paid as soon as you have a horse. So already your horse-buying budget is creeping towards the £2,000 mark!

Other essential items which you will need as soon as you have a horse are saddle (£150 second-hand to £300+ new), girth (£10 plus depending on type), stirrup leathers (£20), stirrup irons (£20), bridle (from £30), bit (from £15), headcollar (from £5), lead rope (£2), complete grooming kit (£25), various buckets and stable tools depending on your chosen method of keeping your horse, and rugs (from £40) depending on time of year. There are also other expenses incurred, but these depend upon the method you have chosen to keep your horse. A closer look at the options is taken in **Finding your horse** — refer to this for a price guide.

You certainly need to do your homework before buying a horse. Why not spend a day looking round the local saddlers and feed merchants, making a note of the costs of feed, hay, straw, tack and so on? It will give you a clear idea of your financial targets.

Stabling costs

Before you find a horse, make sure you can have a suitable home arranged for the new arrival. Facilities vary a great deal from area to area and in some places it is extremely difficult to find grazing, so keeping a horse in full livery (the most expensive option) could be the only possibility. Prices — and facilities — can also vary considerably, so it is worth shopping around well in advance. Ask at your local saddler's or feed merchants for the addresses and telephone numbers of people supplying grazing or livery facilities. Riding club contacts can also help, and a search of the local newspaper's equestrian columns may supply a few leads. The options you come across could include any of the following.

Full livery

This means that your horse's every need is looked after by someone else. Naturally this is a more expensive way of keeping your own horse,

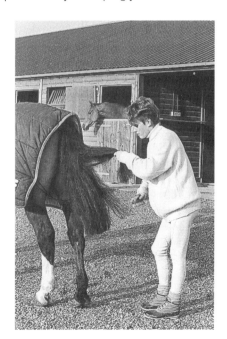

If you keep your horse at full livery, services include grooming.

but for people with hectic working lives it is usually the only way they can entertain the idea of having their own horse.

Prices per week can be £45 to at least £60, according to the locality. This type of service may be provided in a small private yard where a few liveries are taken in to help subsidize the yard owner's horses and competitive career, in larger competitive yards or in riding schools. There are also some yards which are run solely as livery yards, for instance in hunting counties.

The standard of full livery care varies, and you need to check carefully to establish exactly what you are paying for. Your horse should be stabled, mucked out, groomed, exercised by competent riders, fed properly, his tack cleaned and every care taken to ensure that his welfare is catered for. It may be that the horse is made ready for you whenever you wish to ride.

Farrier's costs are additional to full livery, but check whether clipping, plaiting and trimming are extra. It is also advisable to discover exactly who will be riding your horse and how much exercise he will be given. Find out how often he will be turned out in a field to relax and play: for the well-being of your horse it is best for him to have some time out every day.

When investigating a livery yard look carefully at the other equine occupants. Are they well-covered with flesh? Do they appear happy and interested in life? What about their stables? Are the loose boxes large enough for the occupants? Is the bedding clean and adequate? Is the horse's environment a safe one or are there hazards, such as protruding nails, broken windows, rolls of barbed wire in the fields, broken-down gates and poor fencing? Watch the way staff handle the animals, too — each horse is an individual and should be treated as such, not as an expendable machine.

Talk to other owners who use the yard — try to discern if their ideals of horse care match yours and see which areas of the livery they are unhappy about. Both you and your horse need to be happy. If the horse's basic needs are met, what about other facilities? Is there an indoor or outdoor riding area you can use? Are the jumps available for use? Does use of these facilities add to your livery charge? In theory, use of the facilities should be inclusive, but it is always worth checking.

Look at the situation of the livery yard. Are there any bridleways or quiet roads within easy reach? Will you have to ride on or cross major roads? If so, it is even more important that your horse is well-behaved in traffic and that you have experience of road riding. It is worth taking the British Horse Society riding and road safety test as soon as you can.

If you find a good livery yard you will be able to keep your horse well whilst learning a great deal yourself as there will always be someone on hand with advice. You may have to sign a livery agreement, so read it carefully. Usually the purpose is to ensure that a month's

A top class livery yard providing the best for your horse also means peace of mind for you.

written notice is given either way if the livery arrangement proves to be unsatisfactory.

Part livery

This may be available in riding schools. Basically the horse is kept at livery, but the fee is reduced because the animal is used by the school, for example in lessons and to take out hacks.

With some horses and some centres it can work well, but you *must* clearly establish the ground rules. For instance, how much work will your horse be expected to do every day? What standard of rider will be partnering him? How will the horse's work schedule fit in with when you want to ride him? Riding schools tend to be busiest at weekends, just when you will also have more time to ride!

You need to check your insurance liabilities carefully, because it is quite possible that someone could have an accident when riding your horse. Look at the small print on insurance policies, too. It has been known for a company to offer tack insurance only if the tack is kept in a place where fewer than five horses are stabled!

DIY livery

With this arrangement you simply pay for the use of a stable, grazing and facilities and then do all the work yourself. You may be able to come to an arrangement with the yard owners for them to turn out your horse and bring him in from the field, but this will often incur an extra charge. However, in such yards there are usually other livery

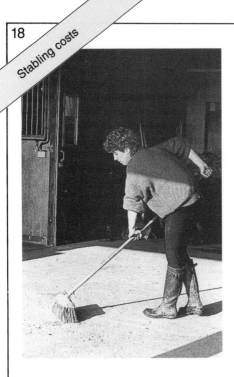

Owning a horse means more than just having an animal to ride — there are lots of jobs associated with keeping one.

owners who need help and by joining together and organizing a rota system you can arrange for all the horses to be cared for while some owners have a night off.

The quality of such yards varies a great deal, and while some have excellent facilities others are very basic with limited grazing and no other riding areas. Prices should reflect the amenities, but you should expect to pay from £10 per week.

Grass livery

Many ponies are kept at grass livery, ie, they live out all year round. This is the cheapest form of livery, whereby for a small sum your animal is kept in a field. Some farmers will rent out a field whilst riding schools and livery yards also offer this option, but often only for ponies, not horses. Check the situation in your local area.

There are disadvantages in not having access to a stable, if, for instance, your horse is ill and needs to be kept inside. Some horses are simply not suited to living outside in winter conditions, so you must take your horse's living arrangements into consideration before you buy any animal. In addition you need to be 100 per cent sure that the field is as secure as it can possibly be. Horse theft is an unfortunate reality, so for your own peace of mind you need to find as safe a home as possible for your new horse.

Finding a decent establishment which can provide all you need,

at a sensible price, is a difficult task. That is why you need
to begin this search in advance of buying your horse, and
it is sensible to take a critical look at the facilities on offer at
various places. For example you may find yourself in this situation:

Place A — a farm which offers DIY livery. Six stables plus one large
field. Very few bridleways close by and major roads have to be crossed
or negotiated to reach quieter roads. No storage space for feed or
tack. Hay and straw is available from the farmer but the quality is not
very good. Grazing is limited for part of the year as the farmer takes
hay off the field which the horses use. Horses have been kept on the
same field continuously for several years and the grazing is rather poor.
Other owners do not attend at the yard every day. Stables rather small.
Security of field questionable. Although the farmer lives on site he is
not interested in horses. A five-minute car journey from home. Cost
is £10 per week, with hay available at £1.50 per bale and straw at 75p
per bale.

Place B — a riding school which offers just full livery. A 25-minute car
journey from home. Decent size boxes, close to bridleways, very little
roadwork, use of indoor school and a few jumps. Horse would be
ridden by student instructress. Close inspection reveals that the
standards of horse care are not ideal — bedding is only just adequate,
horses are fed the bare minimum and a chat to another livery owner
reveals that the horses are not turned out every day. Very few of the
school horses show much of an interest in life, and the staff and owner
are rather rough in their handling of the animals. Cost is £45 per week.

Place C — small private yard which is just three miles from home. Good
stable and grazing, with a field shelter in the three acre field as well
as good, thick hedges. Only one other livery would share the grazing.
sufficient storage space for hay, feed, tack with straw and hay available
from the owner. Situated on a fairly busy road but within easy reach
of quieter roads and bridleways. Knowledgeable horse owners living
on site with someone around the place 24 hours per day. Security
adequate. DIY livery only at £15 per week although for an extra £3
the yard owner would fetch in a horse from the field during the week.

Place D — an isolated yard with four stables and two large fields. No
one lives on site. Small storage space for feed. The three other owners
visit regularly. DIY livery only. Close to good riding country. Gates kept
padlocked. Cost £12 per week.

The above examples do exist and are in close proximity to each other.
In your area there may be an even greater choice, but it is up to you
to find out and then decide what is best for you and your horse. You
may not find your ideal place at first and as you have more years of
experience as an owner under your belt, your expectations of a home
for your horse may change.

Circumstances can also change your requirements. I started off by looking after my own horse, but now work commitments mean I have to keep him in full livery. I could keep him fairly close to home but prefer to undertake a 70 mile round trip every time I want to ride. There is a simple reason for this: the yard where he is now kept provides him with five-star treatment in every respect, and he is loved as one of the family. My horse is happy, and I know that he will *always* receive the very best attention. The peace of mind I have is worth the travelling.

Horse budget checklist

Purchase
Cost of horse
Cost of travelling to see prospective purchases
Cost of vetting
Cost of transporting horse to new home
Cost of insurance

Immediate costs once you become a horse owner
Tetanus/equine influenza vaccination for your new horse
Freeze marking (your horse may already be marked, but if not, it is a wise investment which gives extra peace of mind)
Worming

A freeze brand is a painless way of protecting your horse against horse theft. This horse was marked by Premier Farmkey and his details are held on Farmkey's register.

Right *Hanging water buckets are an alternative to placing buckets on the stable floor where they may be kicked over.*

Below *Corner feeding manger.*

Farrier
Saddle, irons, leathers, girth, numnah
Bridle, bit, martingale (if needed)
Grooming kit
Headcollar and lead rope
Tack cleaning gear

If horse kept at DIY livery
Stable tools, ie, brush, fork, shovel, skip
Haynets

Feed and water buckets
Feed manger
Buckets for field if no trough
Hay
Short feed
Bedding, eg, straw or shavings
Bins for storage of feed — plastic dustbins are fine
Feed scoop
First aid kit

For winter use

New Zealand rug (two if horse kept out all the time)
Stable rug (and blankets if horse fully clipped out. Roller may also be needed dependent upon type of rug)

For summer/travelling

Set of travelling bandages and gamgee or set of travelling boots
Day rug
Anti-sweat sheet
Fly repellent
Fly band (fits on to headcollar or bridle and repels flies)

For competitions and perhaps everyday wear if necessary

Protective boots, eg, brushing, over-reach boots

Costs payable in keeping a horse

(Keep a note of your actual costs every year to help you plan your saving and spending patterns for future years)

Time out in the paddock also allows your horse freedom to let off steam.

Livery or field/stable rent
Hay
Short feed
Bedding
Farriery
Insurance
Routine tetanus and influenza vaccinations
Teeth rasping
Worming
Competition costs, eg, transport, entries
Lessons
Riding club subscriptions
Petrol costs (your everyday cost of getting to your horse as well as extras such as transport to lessons)
Contingency allowance
Repairs fund, eg, to tack, rugs
New equipment fund, eg, for clippers, new rug etc

FINDING YOUR HORSE

The decision has been made, your finances are in order, you know where you are going to keep your horse . . . now all you have to do is to find the right animal! This is where any unsuspecting person can enter a minefield, as buying a horse can be a very risky business. There are people who will sell you a totally unsuitable animal, for example, assuring you that their horse has no vices at all. I know of one person who was sold a 'novice ride' and indeed the animal seemed perfectly quiet and well-mannered. It was only when she got it home and two days had passed that the real animal emerged: a horse who bucked, reared and had only one speed — a flat-out gallop!

So how can you avoid such pitfalls? By not rushing into horse purchase and by asking the advice of a knowledgeable, experienced horsey friend. Through your local riding school or riding club you must know someone who has experience of buying horses. Of course they will not be able to make the purchase decision for you, but they can advise on the advantages and disadvantages of particular animals and offer an unbiased opinion on the suitability of the horse for you. In addition, there will be the expert advice of your vet as to the soundness of the horse for the work it is expected to do.

Now, before you start looking for a horse, think about these questions.

Does the horse's breeding matter?
Your facilities for keeping a horse may affect your choice of animal. For instance native breeds should be content to live out all year round, but a thoroughbred would not appreciate this arrangement.

Could you handle a highly-bred and possibly highly-strung animal? What is the point of having a horse who looks superb but frightens you? Be honest with yourself, and remember that horses are known as great levellers and will soon bring you down to earth (literally!) if you 'over horse' yourself.

How high should the horse be and will he be able to carry my weight easily?
This is where you need the advice of your riding instructress and the

benefit of a knowledgeable person with you when you are looking at horses. Once you know what sort of horse you are after, for instance, a 15hh weight-carrying cob, then don't waste your time or other people's by replying to advertisements for 17hh thoroughbreds.

What age should the horse be?

Novice owners and riders should not be matched with young, inexperienced horses. Although very young animals will be cheaper, remember that they need owners with the time, experience and resources to do them justice. For a first horse you are far better with an older horse who knows his job so that you can learn and gain in confidence. Do not make the mistake of dismissing animals who have reached their early teens — horses often do not come into their prime until they have reached the age of 10.

Does the sex and colour of the animal matter?

This is all a matter of personal preference. If the horse is right for you in all other respects, does it *really* matter whether it's a piebald gelding or a grey mare? You wouldn't refuse to buy a good used car just because of the colour!

What sort of activities am I planning to do with my horse?

Perhaps all you want to do is hack around the countryside in which case a few blemishes on your horse would not be a major problem. However, if you are keen to experience the showing world, then conformation, action, breeding etc would all be important considerations.

If your secret desire is to enter a one-day event, then bear in mind that you may not have the ability to achieve this with your first horse. It is the type of ambition that you can work towards, possibly gaining experience on two or three different horses before you are able to buy the one which will partner you in the fulfilment of your ambition.

Most first-time owners look for an all-rounder — a horse who will jump willingly, be a safe hack, a sensible ride out hunting, good to look after in the stable . . . the type of animal you can have fun on even though it will not necessarily be a star of the show ring.

How much time can I spend looking after my horse?

As mentioned in the first chapter, this will affect the method of keeping your horse, and your corresponding financial commitments. Obviously a horse who is easy to catch, no problem to clip, shoe or load, and free of stable tricks will make horse-owning a pleasure. You will not have to waste time in frustrating activities such as allowing an extra 30 minutes before you ride in order to fetch the horror in from the field!

Does my horse need to be traffic-proof?

Yes, unless, of course, you *never* have to ride on roads and you do not intend to ever sell the horse! For a first-time owner it is best to have an animal who is already trained for riding in traffic.

The degree to which horses are trained can vary, and if necessary you can, with the help of other experienced riders and traffic-proof horses, improve your animal's behaviour on the roads. But the animal may have had a bad experience in the past of which you are unaware and which may explain his traffic problems now. It is therefore sensible for a novice owner to buy an animal who is absolutely reliable in traffic, especially as many riders now have to cope with busy roads.

Buying a horse

So you know what sort of horse you can cope with (in terms of riding and care), you know what you can afford to pay, and you have a clear idea of what you are aiming to do with your horse. Now, where are you going to find him or her? The options are:

Through a reputable dealer Despite all the myths and stories, there are good dealers around who will do their best for their clients. Their livelihood depends on their reputation so it is in their interests to have satisfied customers who will come back again and who will spread the good word amongst the local horsey community. Ask your local contacts for a recommended dealer. Try to find owners who have bought from the dealer and talk to them.

Remember though that the dealer can only sell you a horse — he cannot turn you into a prize-winning rider as well! So it is no good blaming the dealer or your new horse if your lack of preparation and riding ability mean that your first show is a disaster.

An advantage of visiting a good dealer is that there is likely to be a selection of animals available for trial at any one time. You can also ask the dealer if it is possible to exchange the horse if you don't get on with it after three or four weeks. This is often acceptable, although there may be a cash adjustment, particularly if you have managed to spoil the horse to the extent that he needs a lot of time and effort in re-schooling.

The situation is not as unlikely as it sounds. I know of one horse who was a very good and willing jumper, with the potential to win major classes. After two weeks with one particular owner who had lots of money but little understanding of animals, the horse had lost all confidence and was frightened of going near a tiny cross-pole.

If you obtain a written warranty from the dealer that the horse is sound and free from vice, then you should have some comeback under the Trades Descriptions Act if the horse proves to be otherwise. With a private sale you have little chance of any recompense.

Privately in reply to advertisements in your local news-papers (most have horses and saddlery columns) or national equine press. Beware of the same telephone numbers appearing time and again for different horses — some people who deal in horses advertise and sell as if they were private individuals.

'Horses for sale' advertisements can also be found on the notice boards of your local saddlers and in riding club newsletters. You may also hear of prospective purchases via word of mouth, so keep in touch with riding and pony club secretaries, riding school owners and horsey friends.

If you buy a horse who is known locally you should know or be able to find out something of its history. Remember when buying from friends that not everything about the horse is revealed (albeit unintentionally) and so you could put a good friendship at risk.

If you buy from a riding school do not expect your favourite mount to be just the same once you take him away from his usual environment. They often change character — some become much livelier, others are very nappy (ie disobedient) when away from their pals.

From a reputable auction Although many people buy very good animals from sales it is not the best way for a novice to obtain his or her first horse. The reputable auctions will have better quality and more expensive animals and so many people make the mistake of going to the smaller, less reputable sales in the hope of finding a 'bargain'. In reality they land themselves with a costly burden.

If you do buy from an auction you can have the animal vetted by the vet in attendance or arrange for your own vet to check the horse as soon as you have the animal home. Usually, if the horse fails the vet, you have 48 hours after buying the horse at the sale to notify the auctioneers that you are returning the animal. However, you need to check the conditions of the sale before purchasing anything. If the animal is sold without a warranty then you have no option to return him if he is unsound.

Look carefully at what is printed in the auction catalogue about each horse and listen to the auctioneer's description when the animal comes into the sale ring. Often what is not included is as telling as the information which is revealed. For instance, a horse may be described as 'good in traffic, to box and shoe'. Clipping isn't mentioned — could that be because the animal is difficult to clip or just that the owner has not had occasion to clip the horse? Find out!

For instance, in an auction an animal described as a riding pony should be manageable by a child of suitable height and weight for the pony and of average riding competence. In addition the pony should be quiet to ride in traffic. A hunter should be sound, quiet to ride and capable of being a hunter — an animal which becomes very excited and dangerous as soon as hounds appear does not fit the bill!

Working on the assumption that you are looking at a horse either privately or at a dealer's yard, what questions should you be asking? What thoughts need to be going through your mind?

If you telephone in reply to an advertisement you need to establish whether it is worth seeing the horse. Check the details given in the advert, eg, height, breed, sex, and ask for more information. Is the horse good in traffic? If the owner says that she only rides around the bridleways in her area make a mental note — could that be because the horse isn't traffic-proof? Ask if the horse is good to box, clip and shoe. Is the animal well-behaved in the stable? Is it easy to catch? Is the horse a novice ride? What bit is it normally ridden in? Who usually rides the horse? How often? When did the horse last compete? What sort of competing? How successful was it? Has the animal had any serious illnesses or injuries? Is it open to a vet?

If you are satisfied with the replies, arrange a time to visit. Don't be surprised if the owner asks you a few questions, too; any caring owner will be interested in the person who may buy his or her horse. Remember to leave your telephone number with the vendor so that if there are any problems about the arranged visit you can be contacted.

When you contact a dealer tell him what you are looking for and give him an idea of your price range. He may have something which you can see and try, or you may have to wait to be contacted.

Trying horses

The first rule is to take along someone who has more knowledge and experience of horses than you have. Secondly, go along with an open mind, ie, don't be convinced that this is bound to be *the* horse.

Do not be too keen to ride or handle the horse yourself, because by simply observing the horse you can learn a great deal. How does the horse react in the stable? Is he alert and interested or is he nervy and worried about the presence of humans?

Let the owner go in and put a headcollar on the animal, then ask if the horse can be brought out, walked and trotted up. What is the horse's attitude like? Is he lazy or does he move forwards willingly and freely? Now pay attention to the way he moves. Is he a straight mover? Watch carefully as he moves towards you and away from you to see if he brushes, throws out his feet or is pigeon-toed.

Stand back and look at the horse to assess his make and shape. See the points listed under conformation on pages 31-34 for help.

If everything is agreeable so far, ask the owner to tack up the horse, remembering to watch how the animal reacts. Does he accept this everyday job gracefully or is it something of a struggle to get the bit in his mouth? (If this is the case, the reason could be rough handling by the present or past owners.) Does the owner have to move swiftly in order to avoid being bitten when the girth is tightened?

Let the owner ride the horse first. Is the horse obedient and willing, making smooth transitions when asked, slowing down just as easily as moving up a gear? When the horse is warmed up, ask for him to be popped over a few fences and look at the horse's attitude to jumping. Is he keen but sensible in his approach? Does he rush his fences? Is the rider really having to work to get the horse over a small fence? It is also worth moving a couple of fences and rebuilding them elsewhere in the field, so the horse has to jump away from the field gate, for example.

If at any point you decide the horse is not for you, then let the vendor know as tactfully as possible, to avoid any further time-wasting. If you are interested in the animal then it is your turn to ride. Work on the flat, making transitions, riding circles, asking for canter strike-off, lengthening and shortening the horse's stride. When you feel confident pop over a few jumps, including uprights and spreads, jumping towards and away from 'home'.

If you still like the horse ask to see the owner riding it in traffic. Ask to see the horse being loaded into a trailer and being caught up from the field.

Find out as much as you can about the horse's previous experiences at shows, when travelling and out hunting. Try to establish exactly why the horse is being sold. The reason may be perfectly genuine although 'the daughter's lost interest/outgrown the horse/is going off to college' can disguise a whole host of real reasons for sale.

Take time to discuss the horse with your adviser out of the vendor's earshot. If you both feel the horse is right for you then you can discuss the price with the seller, making it clear that you are interested in buying the horse subject to the animal being given the all clear by your vet.

Of course you do not have to decide on the spot whether you would like to buy the horse, and in fact it is often better to go away and think the matter over. If you do this then please let the vendor know your decision — even if it is not to buy the horse — as this is only courteous.

It is unlikely that you will find your horse immediately, but going to see several should help you to make a more informed and rational choice. The search for your horse could take weeks, but remember that you are trying to find a partner who will be with you for some years, possibly for the duration of the horse's life, so you need to do all you can to ensure the right decision is made. You are going to be spending a lot of time with this horse and devoting a lot of money to its upkeep, so it is vital to find a horse that suits you and which you really like.

Vetting

The next stage of horse purchase is the vetting. Do not let the vendor arrange this for you, but ask your own vet to carry out an examination and make sure you are present for the whole procedure.

Before your vet starts to examine your prospective purchase some details will be required from you and the vendor. He or she will want to know what the horse has done in the past and what you intend doing with the animal in the future. Remember that the vet is working for you and is trying to discover if the horse is suitable for the purpose for which it is intended.

The vet will start the examination of the horse in the stable, beginning at the head, checking the horses's ears, mouth and teeth and making a note of the animal's age. In a darkened stable the vet uses an ophthalmoscope to check the horse's eyes both externally, for signs of infection or injury, and internally for any defects or cataracts. The throat and larynx are also checked for any abnormalities.

Then the horse is brought out of the stable and walked on a level surface. This enables the vet to inspect the horse from a distance in order to establish the horse's general condition, and compare one side of the horse with the other to pinpoint any peculiarities of conformation.

A detailed examination of the horse's neck, back and body then follows. The vet feels for any lumps, scars or signs of disease, taking careful note of any unusual reactions which may indicate trouble brewing.

For the next stage quiet is needed, as the vet listens to the horse's heart and lungs at rest. It is not easy to hear a pulse through a stethoscope when a would-be owner is firing questions at you!

Attention is then turned to the horse's legs. All four will be carefully examined, joints are flexed and tendons are gently picked up through the skin so that any previous injuries can be detected. A special instrument is used to examine the feet, to investigate the shape, condition and texture of the hooves. Normally the horse's shoes are left on during this process, although your vet will remove them if asked and provided the vendor gives permission.

The horse is then walked and trotted up in hand. The vet's assistant or the vendor may do this. If you are involved remember that when you turn you should turn the horse's head away from you, not pull him round towards you. This will help the horse's balance. Make sure the horse has sufficient rope so that his head is free and he can move naturally.

As well as indicating whether the horse has any signs of lameness, this walking and trotting up gives the vet the chance to note the horse's way of moving. For instance, the animal may dish or move very closely behind.

Once more attention returns to the horse's legs. Each leg will be held up in turn, the joints flexed and then the horse trotted away as soon as the leg is released. On the back legs you may hear this examination referred to as a 'spavin test'. The purpose of all this is to discover whether there are any problems brewing.

Following this the horse will be tacked up ready for the ridden part of the vetting procedure. At first the animal is walked and trotted in a straight line and then worked on a circle. The vet will stand in the middle of the circle so he can watch the rider working on both reins and listen to the horse. Every so often the horse's heart and lungs are checked. The work-out also includes canter work when again the animal's heart and lungs are examined. During this session the horse will be galloped past and close by the vet so that he can hear if there is any obstruction to the horse's breathing when the animal is exerted.

Some diseases only become apparent after hard exercise, so once the horse is blowing he is pulled up and his heart and lungs examined. The horse is then cooled off and returned to the stable.

A further check will be carried out in 30 minutes' time — the vet will probably use this time to fill in the diagrammatic section of the veterinary certificate. White markings such as socks, stars, etc are all marked down on the certificate as are distinctive features such as whorls, brands and freeze-mark numbers.

After half an hour the horse is examined for stiffness and his heart and lungs are checked. He will be trotted up in hand and turned in tight circles on both reins. His limbs and feet will also be re-examined for any swelling or heat.

Any abnormalities which have been found will be marked on the veterinary certificate. These will include minor points which may not affect the animal's suitability for purchase. Your vet will tell you whether the horse has passed the examination or not. If it has, then you can arrange for the sale to be completed. If not, then you can discuss the areas where the horse has failed with your vet. Of course, if you wish you can ignore the vet's comments and still purchase the horse. It is your decision, but remember that you will have to live with and be responsible for the consequences, whatever they may be.

Conformation

How a horse is put together is important, because poor conformation means a horse is more susceptible to injury and unsoundness as well as being less able to perform some of the tasks he may be asked.

Just as there are many variations of the human form so there are lots of different equine forms. This variety is of course beneficial; in the horse world there is a demand for weight-carrying cobs, super-fast racehorses, jumpers able to tackle huge courses, animals with speed and stamina for long distance events and so on. What may be a weakness of conformation as far as some equestrian disciplines are concerned, may not be a problem at all in another branch of the horse world.

Points of the horse

Although the perfect horse does not exist there are some thoughts or guidelines on conformation which apply to any horse and which can add to or detract from the animal's performance.

Developing an eye for a horse and appreciating the many subtleties of a horse's make and shape is not something which can be taught via a book. Indeed some people have been involved with horses for years and yet still do not seem to be able to 'see' a good horse. You can only start to appreciate conformation by studying horses — and lots of them! Guidance from a more experienced person will also help in pointing out the various pluses and minuses of different horses' conformation. If you take an experienced horse person along with you to view any prospective purchase, they should be able to help distinguish between animals who have conformation faults and those who are under-developed perhaps through immaturity, incorrect work or feeding.

By looking at the successful horses in the various equestrian disciplines you will be able to build up an understanding of why particular aspects of make and shape are so important to the different sports. For example, on a very simplistic level, a successful jumper must have powerful, well-put-together hindquarters and hindlegs.

Your first impression of a horse is important. Does the animal look in proportion? Whatever his breeding the animal should look well-balanced and as if he is one animal, ie, his head and neck should be in proportion to the rest of his body, his legs should look as if they are capable of carrying the horse's body and so on.

A horse should stand square with his weight evenly distributed so that his base of support, ie, the place where his four feet stand, is a rectangle. If there is any deviation from this, eg, one toe is turned in so the base of support is not a true rectangle, then extra strain will be placed on one part.

Look at the horse's topline, that is the proportions of his neck, back and rump. Ideally a horse would be the same length from his poll to his withers and from the withers to the loin. The distance from the loin to the tail would be about three-quarters the length of the poll to wither proportion.

A crucial aspect of any horse's conformation is how the head and neck are set on to the body, because the head and neck act as a balancing pole. Imagine a horse with a large head, a long neck and a low head carriage; this is going to put extra weight on the horse's forehand which in turn puts extra strain on the front legs and shoulders.

Your horse's head does not have to be extremely beautiful, and unless you are interested in showing, it does not matter too much if

A lovely, kind thoroughbred head.

the horse's head is plain. It is more important that the head is well set on to the neck and that the horse is not too thick through the throat. This is because horses with a thick gullet find it difficult to carry their heads properly and when there is flexion at the poll the animal's breathing may be restricted.

Look for a pleasing head, with plenty of breadth between the eyes which should be large and kindly. 'Piggy' eyes often indicate a meaner temperament. The nostrils need to be large to ensure adequate extension during hard work.

A horse needs a strong, neatly set neck to enable him to carry his head correctly. Some horses' necks look poor because of insufficient muscle development. Thin necks which curve upwards are known as ewe necks: as a result the horse has a hollow outline which you will not be able to correct.

Although the neck should be a convex arc, coming smoothly out from the shoulders and withers, avoid horses with too heavy a crest as they generally find it difficult to lighten their forehand and are usually very strong horses to ride.

The slope of the horse's shoulders is important. The shoulders act as shock absorbers and if they are too upright then their efficiency will be reduced, leading to concussion problems in the forelegs and feet. The horse's stride will also be shorter and choppy, so he will not be as comfortable to ride as a horse with a good slope from the point of shoulder to the withers.

Look at horses from the front. There should be plenty of room between the front legs indicating that there is adequate heart and lung space, too. From a side view the horse's rib-cage should be well-sprung, ie, his body appears full and round. An animal which seems to have straight ribs and a flat side would have only restricted space for his heart and lungs.

A relatively short, strong back is preferable, and the loin, which is the link between the quarters and trunk, should also be short and strong. The hindquarters of a horse are often described as the horse's engine for it is here that the propulsive power originates. The quarters need to be strong and well-muscled.

The hindlegs are also an important part of the horse's 'engine power', especially the hocks, as weakness here may affect the horse's 'driving ability'. The horse will not be able to bring his hindlegs underneath him to maximum effect so some of the driving power of his quarters will be lost.

Viewed from the side the hocks should be virtually square in shape with the point of the hock well defined. 'Cow hocks', ie, when the hocks turn inwards when viewed from behind, are a sign of weakness.

Colours and markings of horses

Colours

In order to establish the true colour of a horse you need to look at its points, ie, the muzzle, tips of the ears, mane, tail and legs. Good horses come in all colours, so do not be put off trying a chestnut mare simply because popular lore has it that such mares are fiery characters.

There are four main horse colours — black, brown, bay and chestnut, but within each colour there are variations.

Bay Always has black points but the body colour may be very dark brown (when they are known as dark bays) or a reddish brown (when they are referred to as light bays).

Black Black coat and black points. The animal may have some white markings, eg, a star.

Brown Can be confused with bays. The secret is to check the horse's points. If the mane, tail, muzzle etc are brown then the horse is described as brown.

Chestnut The coat is a bright reddish-brown and the mane and tail may be either flaxen-coloured, lighter or darker than the coat colour. Within the coat colour there are variations, so a chestnut could be a light, dark or liver chestnut.

Dun The colour associated with ancient breeds. It can vary from a golden colour to a rather mousey shade, and is usually accompanied by black points and there may be 'zebra' marks on the legs and a dorsal stripe.

Grey As white is not a colour but a lack of pigmentation, there are a number of terms to describe grey horses according to the variation in pigment. If black hairs are more predominant than white hairs in the coat the horse is an iron grey; if the dark hairs grow in tufts the animal is described as a flea-bitten grey.

With increasing age, the coat of a grey horse becomes whiter, but the horse is always described as a grey, not as a white horse.

Piebald Large, irregular, well-defined patches of black and white.

Roan The term used for a horse with a mixture of two colours in his coat, eg a strawberry roan has chestnut and white hairs throughout his coat.

Skewbald Large irregular patches of white plus any other colour except black.

Markings

Star White mark on forehead which does not have to be the shape of a star!

Snip Small white mark between or on one or the other of the nostrils.

Stripe Narrow white line running down the face.

Blaze Broad band of white running down the face extending over the bones of the nose.

White face The white extends further than with a blaze, taking in the forehead, eyes, nose and part of the muzzle.

Wall eye Can appear unsightly, but it is just that the colouring of the iris is white or blue white.

Leg markings These are generally named according to the part of the leg they affect, eg, white heels or pasterns.

Stockings With a full stocking the white marking extends right up the leg. If it reaches just the knee or hock then it is known simply as a stocking.

Socks White extends to half-way up the cannon bones.

Ermine Term used for black spots on white markings.

White hairs Patches of white hair in the saddle or wither area are usually signs of an old injury.

Sex

Colt An ungelded male under four years of age.

Filly A young female horse or pony under four years old.

Gelding A castrated male horse or pony.

Mare A female horse or pony over four years of age.

Stallion An ungelded male horse or pony over four years of age. Entire is another term used to denote an uncastrated male.

Horsey terms used in advertisements

hh eg, 14.2hh, signifies the height of the animal. Horses and ponies are measured in hands. One hand is equivalent to four inches. In this example the animal is 14 hands and 2 inches high. The measurement is taken as a perpendicular line from the highest point of the withers to the ground. A pony is an animal measuring under 14.2hh; over this height and it is a horse.

BSJA British Show Jumping Association. Horse may be described as 'affiliated BSJA jumper' or have '£xx BSJA winnings'.

HT Hunter trial

NPS National Pony Society. Usually an advert would say 'Reg NPS'.

ODE One-day event

PBA Part-bred Arab

PC Pony Club

PPC Prince Philip Cup. This is a major competition in the world of mounted games, and ponies who show potential in gymkhanas may be described as 'a future PPC pony'.

RC Riding Club

Rising X yrs eg, rising 10 means that the pony is almost 10 years old.

SJ Show jumping

WHP Working hunter pony

XC Cross-country

STABLED HORSES

Stabling is the most time-consuming way of keeping horses but as facilities vary in different areas this may be the only option open to you. If you are looking after your horse yourself then this method involves a great deal of commitment as your day will have to revolve around your horse's needs.

Of course there are advantages in keeping a horse stabled. He will be handy whenever you want to ride, should be easier to keep clean, can usually be kept fitter than a grass kept horse and you have more control over his diet.

However, you should not keep your horse stabled for 24 hours, seven days a week, with the only break being when he is ridden. All horses need time out in a field simply to relax and enjoy themselves, so you should allow your stabled horse a couple of hours' freedom per day. Many owners use what is known as the combined system of horsekeeping, ie the horse spends some time out and the rest of the time stabled. It is a flexible system with the amount of time out varying according to the weather, time of year and circumstances.

> Horses appreciate holidays just as much as you do. A change of environment and a rest will be appreciated by your horse.

If you are in the unfortunate position of being able to rent just a stable with no grazing, then you should split your riding sessions into two and lead the horse out in hand to graze on verges. This will split up the horse's day more. A small area, even if it is a yard rather than a grazing paddock, would be useful just to turn the horse loose. In the meantime, try to find alternative living arrangements for your horse as being confined to a stable is not a healthy long-term prospect.

Stables

As you are looking around for a suitable home for your horse, you will notice that people's definitions of stables vary from superb, roomy loose boxes to tumbledown sheds which would be more suitable as bonfire material than homes for animals! So what criteria should your stable meet?

For a horse, a stable should be at least 12 ft by 14 ft (3.7m × 4.3m) and for ponies 10 ft by 12 ft (3m × 3.7m). The doors should be 8 ft (2.4m) high by 4 ft (1.2m) wide and split into two portions. You should be able to hook the top door back to provide ventilation; if the door is just pushed back then it can swing about and frighten or injure the horse. The lower door needs to be high enough to prevent the horse jumping or climbing out over it (this can be a pretty frightening sight).

Stable doors should open easily and open out into the yard. It is dangerous if they open into the stable, since if the horse were to become trapped across the doorway it would be impossible to open the door to get to him. Latches on the doors must be strong and without any projections which could injure a horse. The bottom door should have two latches, with the bottom one being foot-operated to save you constantly bending down to open it. Some horses are very adept at opening their stable doors and just providing one latch at the top of the stable door makes escape easy for equine Houdinis!

Ventilation is very important in stables. A constant supply of pure air is needed by the horse's body to help it resist diseases. Stuffy atmospheres are not healthy, but neither are draughty stables. Natural

The top half of stable doors should be fastened back so the occupant can look out of his stable without any danger of the top door blowing shut and frightening him.

Right Foot-operated latches at the bottom of stable doors are very convenient.

Below A safe stable window, with bars between the glass and the horse.

roof ventilation will be provided by stables with sloping roofs which also offer plenty of air space and light.

Stable windows are also needed as inlets for fresh air, but they must be protected with bars so that the horse cannot damage himself. The lower edge of the window needs to be 8 ft (2.4m) from the floor and the window should be hinged so that it opens with an inward slant. Windows should be on the same side as the door. If there are windows opposite the door as well, you must be careful to prevent draughts.

Check that the roof of your stable is not leaking, where tiles or slates have been broken. Galvanized iron is not a particularly good roofing material as it does not encourage an equable temperature. In summer

Left *How NOT to hang a haynet — a horse could easily catch his foot in this.*

Below *To ensure a haynet is tied at a sensible height, thread the tie through the tying-up ring and then through the bottom of the net. Pull the tie up to the top of the net before securing.*

Left *The end result should be a net tied at a reasonable height for the horse to be able to pull at, but which is still at a safe height once the net has been emptied. Never tie a net so high that a horse has to stretch up to pull at the hay.*

the stable will be very hot and in winter very cold, so if it is used there should also be an inner roofing of wood.

The stable floor is also important. If it is concreted then it should not be slippery, and should be without huge ridges which could cause injury. There should be a slight slope from the front to the rear of the box to allow for drainage.

Stables should be sound, solid constructions, sited so that there is plenty of light and air whilst providing shelter from the prevailing winds. Your stable should not be overshadowed by other buildings which inhibit the supply of light and air. Neither should it be part of a small enclosure, as such arrangements help the spread of contagious disease.

Any fittings inside the stable should be designed so that the risk of injury to the occupant is reduced; mangers, for instance should have well-rounded corners and be fitted at least 3 ft 6 in (1.1m) above the ground. Tying-up rings should be firmly fitted. Hay-racks fitted above the horse's head level would be better removed, because they cause the horse to feed in an unnatural way and there is the danger of the hay-seeds falling into his eyes. The fewer the fittings in a stable the better.

Hooks for headcollar and bridle on the outside of the stable, plus a latch for holding back the lower door — this ensures that it cannot be caught by the wind and blown into the horse as he is being led into or out of his stable.

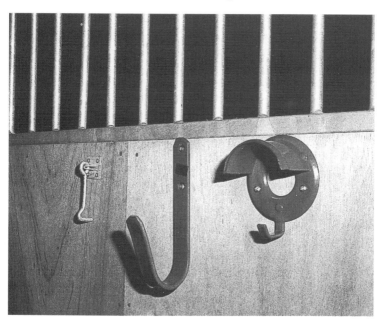

Light switches are better positioned outside the stable, well away from the reach of the horse. Wherever they are, light switches should have adequate protection so that there is no risk of electrocution.

Check your potential stable for any projecting nails or wood which could cause injury, and make this a regular part of your routine so that any hazard can be rectified before it has chance to reach its potential! Fire extinguishers should be kept on hand in a stable yard. Make sure you know where they are sited and how to use them.

If you are in a position to build your own stable at home then it would be wise to seek advice in respect of requirements from your solicitor rather than going straight to the local planning authority. This should ensure that the advice given is for your benefit.

Bedding

Your horse will need a deep, clean bed in his stable. Do not skimp on bedding, because if you provide only a thin layer of bedding material your horse will not be able to lie down without injuring his elbows and hocks. He will be uncomfortable, there will be no warmth provided, he will be lying in his own urine and excreta, there will be more chance of him becoming cast (ie, stuck on his back) and he could easily slip and injure himself when getting up, lying down or stretching out to stale.

The bed should be deep enough so that when the prongs of the fork are pushed into the bed they do not hit the ground and make a clonking noise. The walls of the bed need to be banked up all around, that is at a higher level than the rest of the bed. Every time you add new bedding shake out the new material thoroughly.

Bedding materials

Straw or shavings tend to be the most commonly used bedding. There are three types of straw, wheat, oat and barley, with wheat straw generally considered to be the best for bedding down horses. This is because it is durable and is not usually eaten. Oat straw also makes good bedding but horses often eat it, while barley straw can contain awns which can irritate the horse. Old straw which has been stored well is generally better than new straw as it is dryer and more elastic. If you have the storage space it is cheaper to buy straw in bulk off the field.

Shavings are becoming more widely used, and are generally available in bales or bags. Some people save money by obtaining shavings direct from local wood mills, but you need to be very careful that no foreign bodies are contained in such shavings. If your horse eats his bed when on straw, then switch to shavings.

Some horses have respiratory problems which are not helped by

Tidying up a shavings bed.

being bedded on straw. Shavings or better still, paper bedding, should be used.

Mucking out

This is the name given to the thorough cleaning of your horse's bed when the dirty and soiled bedding is removed and the clean bedding is piled up so that the stable floor can be dried and aired.

Ideally this should be done every day but if you are a working owner with limited time this may not always be possible. You may therefore decide to skip out your horse every day, removing the dirty and wet bedding and replacing it with clean bedding, but reserving a full mucking out for the weekend when you have more time.

Alternatively, you could use what is known as a deep litter system whereby dirty and wet bedding is removed every day, new bedding added as required but the whole bed is not disturbed by a thorough mucking out for a couple of months. Then the whole bed is removed and the process starts again. Whichever method you use here's how to muck out.

Collect together your equipment, a broom, fork, shovel, wheelbarrow, headcollar and rope. Tie up your horse inside the stable or — and this is preferable as it will speed up the process — turn him out or put him in another stable.

Mucking out

Mucking out tools should be stored neatly in a safe place, away from the inquisitive lips of any horses!

Place the wheelbarrow in the doorway. Remove any droppings from the stable. Then systematically working through, toss up the bedding, separating the wet and soiled bedding and depositing this in the barrow along with the droppings. Throw the clean bedding up along one side of the stable. Sort all the bedding in this way, transferring the dirty material to your muck-heap. Sweep your stable floor and if possible leave the clean bedding stacked against the wall so that the floor can dry and air.

When you lay the bed again, spread the clean bedding around, mixing in new bedding to ensure that the horse has a good deep bed. Bank up the walls and provide adequate bedding around features such as mangers so that your horse does not bang a leg if he becomes excited when feeding. Leave a clear space for the water buckets.

If you use shavings it is often easier and quicker to equip yourself with rubber gloves and pick up the droppings.

The muck-heap should be positioned away from the stables. Bear in mind any houses overlooking your stables as you do not want to give neighbours cause for complaint. Try to keep your muck-heap compact by trampling it or using shovels to beat it down, as this will assist the decomposition of the manure. The manure should be removed regularly. The owner of your livery yard may already have an arrangement with a local farmer or may offer the manure for sale to gardeners. Shavings are generally burnt.

Stabled horse — a suggested routine

If you are a working horse owner, you need to establish a routine which is suitable for your horse and which also fits in comfortably with your life. Listed below is a routine I used to cope with looking after my horse myself whilst working a regular 9–5.30 week. The horse was stabled 10 minutes' drive away from my home. This is included here for you to use as a basis for your routine if you wish. What works for one horse and one individual may not suit anyone else.

Weekday mornings

6 am   Get up (easy in summer; really difficult in winter when it's cold and dark outside!).

6.15   Arrive at stables. Check for anything unusual. Quarter and check over the horse. Tack up and fit boots.

6.30   Ride

7.45   Return from ride, remove bridle, give haynet. Loosen girth, but do not remove saddle for five minutes or so (to let circulation in saddle area return to normal gradually). Remove boots and

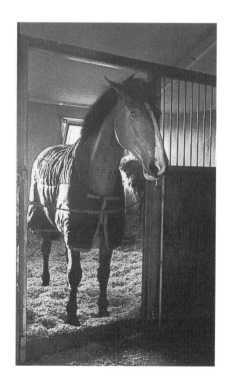

A lead rope across the stable entrance ensures that the horse stays safely inside but you can work in and around the stable without constantly having to open and shut the door.

pick out feet. Give short feed. Check water supply in field. Remove overnight haynet and water buckets from stable. Swill out water and feed bucket. Collect skip, fork, brush and rubber gloves. Skip out stable, depositing soiled bedding on muck-heap. Remove saddle and return tack to car. Fit turn-out rug if needed. By this time horse has generally finished his feed so he can be turned out in the field. Make stable ready, ie, refill and return water buckets, tie up new haynet, put carrots/apples in manger ready for the horse's return from field. (My horse was generally brought in at midday by the yard owner, although weather conditions sometimes dictated less time in the field or the horse being turned out by the yard owner later in the day.) Put stable tools away.

8.15   Leave for home, aiming to leave for work at 8.40. Breakfast at work!

Evenings

6 pm   Arrive home, make up feed.

6.15   Arrive stables. Check over. Feed. Refill haynets for following day. Swill out feed and water buckets. Skip out and add new bedding as required. Groom and pick out feet. Refill water buckets and return. Give night haynet. Tidy yard and storage area.

7.30   Home. Prepare feed and carrots ready for morning. Soak sugar beet.

Weekends

Horse's basic routine the same but additional jobs include:

a Bed thoroughly mucked out and left up while horse turned out so that floor can dry and air.

b Paddock — collect droppings and check fencing, etc.

c Tidy muck-heap.

d Collect supplies of food, hay and bedding.

e Visit to farrier every five weeks.

f Scrub buckets and manger.

g Major tidying session on storage areas.

h Tack taken to pieces and thoroughly cleaned.

i Fit in any lessons/shows.

NB In winter, you need to allow time to change rugs, hang rugs up to dry and air. If you have a field shelter, include time in your weekly schedule to muck out this. Allow extra time in winter for breaking ice in field troughs and distributing hay in your field.

If you have several haynets you can have a major filling and weighing session every three days or so instead of filling nets every day.

Obviously, whether you ride in the morning or evening will be dictated by your individual circumstances and the time of year. Take advantage

Right *Save time by filling haynets for the day or couple of days instead of as and when you need them.*

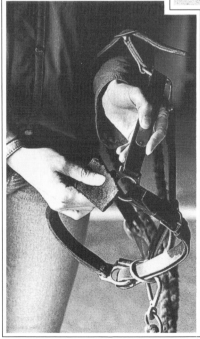

Left *A daily wipe over after use helps to keep your tack in better condition. However, you still need to give your gear a 'proper' clean as well.*

of summer evenings — then you will have some nice memories when you are struggling along in the winter, trying to bounce out of bed at unearthly hours!

Stable vices

Crib-biting/wind-sucking

What it is The horse grabs hold of a projecting object such as a stable door or manger with his teeth, arches his neck and swallows air. Sometimes horses do this without biting on anything (known as wind-sucking). These are serious problems which can lead to colic, impaired digestion, damaged teeth and therefore a reduced ability to graze.

Crib-biting/wind-sucking should not be confused with wood chewing. Lots of horses chew wood (a bad practice which should be discouraged) and this may lead to cribbing. It is the swallowing of air which determines the real crib-biter; as the horse swallows he will gulp or grunt.

Why it occurs Horses which are stabled can easily become bored. Think of how horses in the wild behave: they live in groups, roaming around, playing and eating at will, associating with various horses in their herd as they wish. Our domesticated horses still have the same basic instincts for company of their own kind, time to play and relax etc, but we impose upon them a totally different way of life. It is therefore

It's vital for the health of your horse that he has time to play and relax in the field with his companions.

not surprising that they become bored and take to vices such as crib-biting to fill in the time.

Symptoms Marks on the stable door/manger and the sound of the horse gulping are tell-tale indications. A horse who has been crib-biting for some time will have teeth which show signs of irregular wear.

Action As this habit is addictive it is difficult to eliminate the problem completely, so 'prevention is better than cure' is an extremely apt adage. Think about your stable management routine: are you giving your horse the opportunity to become bored? Is there anything you can do to prevent this? For example, could you give him more but smaller feeds to break up his day? Is he getting enough hay? Could you feed his hay in nets with smaller holes so it takes longer for the horse to pull at the hay? Can the horse be turned out to graze? Perhaps it is worth splitting his grazing into two sessions. Could his exercising be done in two sessions rather than one? Can the horse be moved to a box in a busier part of the yard where there is more to attract and keep his attention?

Established crib-biters can be fitted with cribbing straps. These are collars which are placed around the top of the horse's neck. These do not interfere with the horse's normal breathing, but they pinch when the animal tries to arch his neck to swallow air.

Weaving

What it is This is another manifestation of boredom in the stabled horse. The animal rocks and swings his head from side to side.

Symptoms There are various degrees of weaving, from the horse who leans over his stable door, moving his head a little to the horse who rocks violently from one leg to the other. Some horses weave as they are leaning over a door, others stand in the middle of the stable, weaving away.

Action All the points regarding the reduction of boredom apply. Anti-weaving grilles can also be fitted. These are metal grilles which have a V-shaped section in the middle, and are fitted on the bottom stable door, filling the space above, leaving only the V through which the horse can look out. They prevent the horse from looking over the door and moving his head from side to side.

OUTDOOR HORSES

From a horse's point of view it is more natural to live out where he is free to move around at will, graze as and when he wants, spend time with his companions, roll whenever he wishes and so on. There are advantages for the owner, too, as to some extent the horse is exercising himself and if a day's riding has to be missed the consequences are not as drastic as when a stabled horse is denied his exercise. This does not mean that the grass kept horse will keep himself fit, but his way of life should promote health.

However, living out can also be an ordeal for the horse if his field is inadequate for his needs. Unfortunately it is an all too common sight to see horses and ponies leading miserable existences on tiny pieces of waterlogged land with no food or shelter from the elements. If your horse is going to spend all or part of his time living out then you need to ensure that his home field provides everything necessary for his well-being in a safe environment.

For those of you lucky enough to own your own land you can do a great deal to ensure that your horse has a safe outdoor home. If you are renting a field find the best you can and then negotiate with the owner about providing safer fencing, splitting the field so part can be rested and so on.

One of the big questions is, how much land will my horse need? There are no hard and fast rules as so much depends on the quality of the grazing available, the management of the land, soil type and the system of care which is being applied to the animals using the field. As a minimum, an acre and a half of decent pasture would be sufficient for one horse, but if you have a larger field which can be divided into paddocks then it will be easier to manage the land to greater advantage.

Horses are wasteful grazing animals, selecting the most palatable grasses and rejecting other grasses. This is why many people keep sheep or cattle with horses, or let the paddocks be grazed by other stock. Such animals eat the grass ignored by the horses and also help to reduce the worm parasites.

The subject of pasture management is huge and you would be well

advised to learn all you can. The British Horse Society
has inexpensive booklets on the subject and there are also
books devoted to the subject. You can also get practical help
in the form of soil analysis from fertilizer companies and your local
Ministry of Agriculture, Fisheries and Food. There may be a charge
for the soil analysis, but you will then know whether, for instance, your
land requires lime, potash or nitrogen. Looking after land requires long-
term planning and of course it is much easier if you own the land rather
than being just a grass livery.

If you share land with other liveries — and especially if the area is
a small one — then arrange between you to pick up the droppings
regularly. If they are left they encourage worm infestation and sour the
grass. Consequently the horses will avoid these rank patches and you
will have reduced the amount of grazing available. Chain-harrowing
on a weekly basis is an alternative to picking up the droppings.

Fencing is another important consideration, because if it is inadequate or dangerous your horse could easily injure himself. Post and
rail is the best and most expensive type of fencing. Preferably the
fencing should be around 4ft (1.2m) high.

Natural fencing, in the form of good strong hedges, has the
advantage of providing shelter as well. It is important to carry out regular
checks for weak spots in the hedging and to reinforce with timber where
necessary so the horse cannot push his way through the hedge.
Another point to check with hedging is that it does not contain any
poisonous plants such as yew or deadly nightshade.

Post and wire fencing is often used by horse owners as it is relatively

Safe, well-constructed post and rail fencing.

Above Thick, strong hedges are a good natural source of fencing and shelter.

Left Barbed wire is not a suitable fencing material for horse or pony paddocks.

In wet weather your paddocks can become very churned up — here shavings have been put down to ease the problem.

cheap and is adequate, provided it is properly maintained. The top of the fence should ideally be timber rails with strands of heavy gauge wire beneath. It is vital that the wire is kept taut and the lowest strand should be at least 12 in (30cm) above the ground or your horse could easily put his foot over it. Regular checks are needed to ensure that the staples are secure.

Fences made up of sheep netting, old bits of pallets, barbed wire and anything else which happens to be lying around are *not* suitable for horse and pony paddocks.

> When turning out your horse make sure the gate is closed so that the horse cannot make a break for freedom. Always face the horse towards the gate before you release him — there is less opportunity for him to kick you.

Gates should be wide and swing open into the field, with fastenings kept in good repair; imagine battling with a stubborn lopsided gate whilst trying to hang on to a horse who has just been upset by an inconsiderate motorcyclist screaming past at a tremendous speed!

For security, fit heavy-duty padlocks and chains to both ends of the gate. The area around the gate and any field shelters often becomes churned up in wet weather so a layer of hard core or similar eases the problem.

If you have the chance to erect new fencing at any time try to avoid providing corners, but rather have fencing which curves around. Where there are corners it is easy for a horse to be trapped and kicked by another.

As you walk around your field checking the fencing, keep an eye open for other debris which could be a hazard, such as bottles or cans thrown over by passers-by, household rubbish which may have been dumped, grass cuttings (especially if the field is close to houses), baler twine, dangerous plants and glass. Non-horsey people think they are doing the horse a favour by giving him the cuttings after they have mowed the lawn. However, if your horse's field is close to houses make it clear to residents that cuttings are dangerous to horses and can indeed kill.

Store your jumps away in a corner of the field.

Laburnum in gardens overlooking your field is dangerous to horses as are privet, bracken, laurel, hemlock, foxgloves, box and ragwort. The latter is widespread and it is horrifying to see paddocks all over the country which are homes for horses and ponies and yet are infested with ragwort. This plant is easily recognizable by its woody stems and yellow flowers, and is frequently found on poor pasture. Dangerous

Avoid sharp edges on field troughs — your horse or pony may injure himself.

plants such as ragwort should be pulled up by the roots and burnt. Do not leave such plants lying in the field as some are more dangerous when they are dead than when they are growing. Ask your instructor for help in identifying poisonous plants, visit your reference library or encourage the local riding club to have an instructional lecture on the subject.

Another important consideration for your horse's field is the water supply. He will need a good, reliable supply of clean fresh water. Streams with sandy bottoms do not fit the bill as there is a danger of the horse getting sand colic. Nor are stagnant ponds suitable supplies either and these should be fenced off. Water troughs which are self-filling are good, but the edges of the trough should be smooth so there is less risk of injury to the horse. Chipped old baths are not really suitable. You will need to check the trough daily to clear it of any dirt or leaves which may cause clogging. In winter the ice will have to be broken.

Position the trough so that it is not overhung by trees. It should not be sited so that a horse could become trapped between a trough and the fencing and avoid putting the trough in a corner where a fight may develop between horses.

Scrub out the troughs regularly and check every day that the self-filling mechanism is working. If you have no alternative but to use buckets place them in old tyres to prevent them being knocked over.

Placing water or feed buckets in old tyres ensures that the buckets are not knocked over.

Clean and refill them at least twice a day.

If your field has no natural shelter or shade then you will need to provide some. Horses do not like dark confined areas so any field shelter you erect should be large, light and airy. It needs to be big enough to house all the animals using the field without risk of injury. If the animals are crowded together there is more risk of injury through bullying and kicking. The entrance should be open fronted or very wide to prevent crowding and possibly bullying.

Site your shelter on level, well-drained ground, with the entrance away from prevailing winds. Several firms make shelters and will erect them for you. Choose one which has enough height so that your horse is not discouraged from entering the shelter. An overhanging roof will also provide some shelter and shade for any horse who is distrustful of actually going into the shelter. A field shelter can also be converted into a temporary stable if the need ever arises.

In summer, field shelters provide welcome relief from the sun and flies, and in winter are used as a refuge from the wind and rain. You can provide bedding in the shelter for extra warmth in winter, but remember that it will need mucking out as well!

Some animals have to be accustomed to using shelters, and using them for feeding hay or short feed (concentrated food such as oats and cubes) helps. However, you must always provide enough room between the haynets and bucket feeds to discourage fighting. Provide hay outside the shelter as well.

Wherever you tie haynets make sure they are tied high enough so that when empty there is no danger of the horse getting a leg caught up in the net. If you feed from the ground make sure there is one more pile of hay than the number of horses to ensure that even the timidest horse gets his allocation.

Beware of using hay-racks as used for cattle, because these can present opportunities for your horse to injure himself.

If you share a field with other owners and your visiting times are different then catch your horse and fetch him out of the field in order to feed and attend to him. Otherwise you could find yourself surrounded by curious and hungry onlookers who may become nasty if their feed has not arrived.

When you keep a horse out at grass there are time savings in that you do not have to muck out and bed down a stable but this does not mean that you can reduce your visits to your horse. You will still need to visit at least twice a day, irrespective of the weather or time of the year. Indeed in winter it may be necessary to visit more often, to break the ice on the water supply!

You will need to keep a careful eye on your horse's weight during the spring and summer. Beware of large bellies and pads of fat on the shoulders as laminitis could be around the corner.

Supplementary feeding of, for example, hay and/or short feed may be necessary all year round or only at certain times according to the individual needs of the horse. If your horse can be an awkward customer to catch make sure you get into the routine of catching him up to feed him, as this helps him to realize that being caught can result in pleasant experiences and does not necessarily mean that he has to work.

Remember that he will need to be checked over on each of your visits for any injuries. Your grooming should be restricted to picking out feet, brushing over with a dandy brush, attending to the mane and tail with a body brush, sponging the eyes, nose and dock. If you groom a grass-kept horse too thoroughly you will remove the grease from his coat which he needs as protection against the weather.

Mud fever

Mud fever is a skin infection affecting the horse's lower legs, generally the fetlock and pastern areas, although it can spread further up the legs. It is caused by a germ which loves wet conditions. When a horse has been standing around in a waterlogged field or a muddy paddock then the skin on his legs becomes sodden. This provides an excellent opportunity for the germ to start invading the horse's pores and hair

Fields can soon become quagmires after a spell of wet weather, conditions which are ideal for promoting problems such as mud fever.

follicles. This germ cannot operate on dry skin but on wet skin it can be very virulent.

The germ which causes mud fever also attacks horses whose coats have become absolutely soaked with rain, causing a condition known as rain scald. An obvious preventative method is to provide your horse with a New Zealand rug during the wet months.

Symptoms

In its early stages, mud fever does not cause any apparent problem, but as it spreads it can make the horse's legs very tender and swollen, resulting in lameness.

It first appears as crusty scabs on the surface of the skin. This is why it pays to examine your horse carefully every day so that you can catch any problem in the early stages. These initial signs of mud fever can look like bits of dried mud but if you pick them off, raw patches of skin are revealed.

If you do not catch the problem at this stage evidence of mud fever will manifest itself as the horse's legs will swell and the scabs will crack and ooze.

Action

If the mud fever has reached an advanced stage and your horse is stiff or lame, then call out your vet as antibiotics may be needed.

Hopefully you should have caught any problem at an early stage. Your horse will need to be kept out of the mud so his legs can remain dry and clean. This is where access to a stable is desirable because it is impossible to cure anything like mud fever if the horse has to constantly stand outside.

If there are only a few scabs in an early stage, then keeping the horse in for a few days should clear the condition. However, if there are lots of scabs you need to carefully remove them and apply an antiseptic ointment. The horse's legs must then be kept as dry as possible. If in any doubt, call your vet and seek his advice.

Prevention

Do not constantly wash your horse's legs. It is better to let any mud dry and then brush it off. If you do wash your horse's legs dry them thoroughly afterwards, using old towels. Frequent washing should be avoided as it removes the grease from the coat — the grease is the horse's natural waterproofing system.

Some horses have heavily feathered legs, but it is easier to prevent mud fever and spot any initial problem if the feather (hair) is trimmed.

In wet conditions you can increase the waterproofing of your horse's legs by applying petroleum jelly to the heels and liquid paraffin to the hairier parts of the legs. However, the horse's legs must be dry and free of mud before you apply either of these or you will make things worse.

Worming

It is a fact of life that horses have worms, and if these parasites are unchecked then you are exposing your horse to all kinds of serious problems, including damage to internal organs and colic. Indeed, worms can even result in the death of horses.

It is a great shame that despite easy access to worming powders and pastes, some owners still neglect this essential part of horse management. Worms are dangerous and to overlook their potential effect on your horse is a serious neglect of your duty as an owner.

Every horse has worms. The parasites live in the horse's intestines, where each female worm lays large numbers of eggs which are passed out in the horse's dung. The eggs hatch out on the grass so any paddock which is grazed by horses will have thousands of baby worms on it. The worms cannot be seen by the naked eye. Horses grazing the paddock will therefore eat some of these worms. Once inside the horse the worms mature, breed and produce eggs, so the whole cycle starts again.

As you cannot prevent your horse from picking up worms you need to ensure that the worm infestation is kept under control. A regular worming programme is essential for all horses, although it is generally accepted that it is beneficial to worm grass-kept animals more regularly than their stabled friends. Horses kept at grass should be wormed every six weeks in winter and every month in the summer, ie, May to September. Every three months should be adequate for stabled horses. If you are not sure when you horse was last wormed you can ask your vet to check on the worm infestation. He will analyse a dung sample and advise you.

Wormers are available in paste form, which comes in a syringe from which the paste is squirted into the horse's mouth, or in powder form to mix in with the horse's feed. You will need to change the brand of wormer used so that the parasites do not become resistant.

Apart from worming your horse regularly, you can help control the worm infestation of your grazing by picking up the droppings.

Tapeworms are now known to be associated with certain types of summer colic so it's a sensible precaution to give all grass-kept horses a double dose of Strongid some time between June and August. At the time of writing this is the only wormer, as far as is known, which will be effective against tapeworms.

In winter remember to include Eqvalan in your worming programme to act against bots.

Lice

If your horse starts to scratch himself a great deal, perhaps even rubbing himself raw, it is possible that he has lice. This problem often

Lice occurs with horses living out in groups, and particularly during winter when the animals have long coats.

The lice are generally found under the mane and around the withers, with adult lice passing from one horse to another, quickly infesting their new host. They are difficult to see, although the eggs may be seen on the coat hairs. Lice may also be passed on via grooming kit, which is why you should keep your horse's brushes for his exclusive use.

Louse powder available from a saddler or vet is a cheap and easy way of dealing with the problem. Sprinkle it along the horse's back and neck, rub it in well and then repeat the process every couple of weeks through the winter.

EQUIPMENT

It is astonishing how much equipment a single horse needs, and after a few years as a horse owner you will be amazed at all the bits and pieces you seem to have collected. When you stop to add up the value of your tack, rugs, bandages and so on the total is considerable. However, you can take comfort in the fact that good quality equipment which is well looked after will give many years of service.

Although it is not always easy — because of financial limitations — try to buy the best equipment you can. This is especially important with saddlery. There are some very cheap saddles on the market from India and Pakistan but they are made from inferior materials and generally need replacing within a few months. It is a better investment to buy good quality second-hand saddlery rather than new but poor quality tack. Let us look at the different gear you will need, how it is made and how to recognize good workmanship.

Saddles

There is plenty of choice here. In fact different equestrian disciplines have saddles especially to cater for their needs, such as dressage, show-jumping and racing saddles. With such a variety of horses, ponies and riders, it is not surprising that saddles are made in a wide range of sizes and different widths.

The framework upon which a saddle is built is known as the tree and traditionally this was made from beechwood. However, many modern trees are made of laminated wood, so combining strength and lightness. You will also hear the phrase 'spring tree'; modern saddles have springs, pieces of light steel, running from the front to the rear of the tree on the underside to help to give the seat of the saddle greater flexibility and resilience. Such saddles generally have dipped seats. Older saddles and some other specific saddles such as children's saddles, do not have these springs and are known as rigid-tree saddles.

The front or head of the saddle tree may be cut back which ensures clearance if a horse has particularly pronounced withers.

By its design, a saddle seat should help the rider to sit in the deepest part of the saddle with the rider's legs lying in the correct position on the saddle flap. The seat of the saddle is made by putting pieces of interwoven strips of nylon web or canvas from side to side and front to rear of the tree. These are pulled tight and secured. A piece of leather shaped to form the seat and the saddle flaps is then secured in position.

In order to prevent the tree from coming into contact with the horse's back, saddles have panels stuffed with materials such as wool and generally covered in leather. The panels also help to spread the weight of the rider, but if the panels need restuffing or are badly stuffed, they can cause considerable discomfort to the horse. In between the panels, there is a gap running the length of the saddle which is known as the gullet.

Stirrups are attached to the saddle via the stirrup bars, metal rods attached to the saddle tree, which are best and safest made from forged steel. You will notice a hinged piece on the stirrup bar which should always lie flat when you are riding. If the bar were in the 'up' position, the stirrup would not be able to come off the bar — imagine the horror of a rider being dragged along by a panic-stricken horse.

There are usually three girth straps on a saddle, the first strap being connected to a separate piece of web to the other straps. It is normal practice to use the first two straps for attaching the girth. Behind the girth straps lies the sweat flap which prevents the horse being injured by the girth buckles. A buckle guard is pulled over the girth buckles so that they cannot rub holes in the leather of the saddle flap, ie, the outer flap of the saddle against which the rider's legs lie.

Knee or thigh rolls may be included on the saddle to help the rider maintain seat and leg position.

So how can you tell if a saddle is made from decent leather? If you are buying from a saddler who is a member of the Master Saddlers' Association (he will display the Association badge) then you should be able to rely on his advice and the standard of the tack he stocks. However, if you are buying secondhand or from a sale, you will need other pointers.

Good leather *smells* good; if there is a sickly aroma about the tack there is a fair chance it is a cheaper, poor quality import. Feel the leather; if new it should feel firm and very slightly greasy, not dry. Rub the back of the leather; if it fluffs up then the leather has not been properly treated at the tanning stage. The leather should be smooth textured without any rough or loose fibres. Bend the leather; bubbles should not form on the skin.

If you are buying secondhand, check that the saddle tree is not broken. Take hold of either side of the pommel and push inwards; there will be a very slight amount of 'give' in spring-free saddles but if it is excessive it is possible that the tree is broken. A saddler would be able to advise you, but the cost of replacing a tree can be expensive as

Right Check your tack regularly for weak spots such as this — a stirrup leather suddenly snapping could have disastrous results.

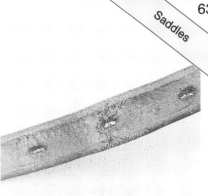

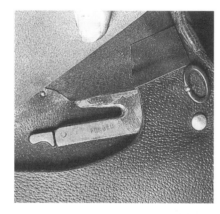

Left Forged steel stirrup bars are safest.

Below A broken saddle tree — note the clean break along the metal plate which formed the pommel of the saddle.

well as time-consuming. It is also wise to check the stirrup bars. If these move it indicates that the rivets fixing them to the saddle tree have become loose.

Check the stitching on all your tack. Better quality saddlery has more stitches to the inch — you would expect about seven to the inch on stirrup leathers and ten to the inch on decent bridlework. If stitching is worn then repairs need to be carried out immediately. Look carefully where leather bends over, for example on stirrup leathers and on bridles, as cracks can appear. Frayed webs, for example on the girth straps, could result in a nasty accident, so check a saddle thoroughly, and remember that the cost of repairs may outweigh the seemingly cheap price of a used saddle.

Stainless steel fittings are safer and easier to maintain than nickel or nickel plate which can become distorted or snap.

If you do buy second-hand saddlery or horse clothing, it is sensible to disinfect the items before use, to reduce the possibility of contagious skin diseases being passed on. In addition, leather which has been mouldy may still contain nasty spores which could result in skin infections for your horse. Sterilising fluids can be bought at chemists.

If you buy a new saddle, it will certainly not come complete with stirrup leathers, irons and girth. The position may vary with a used saddle. Stirrup leathers can be bought in different lengths and thicknesses; remember that all new leather stretches and it is wise to swap your leathers around as otherwise the leather on the nearside, from which you mount, will stretch most.

Stainless steel irons are best, with rubber treads fitted to prevent the foot slipping and to act as insulation for your feet. Irons which are too small are dangerous as your foot may be caught in the stirrup and you could be dragged. Equally, your foot could slip through an iron which was too large. Allow ½ in (12mm) clearance at either side with the broadest part of your foot in the stirrup.

Girths come in a variety of materials and styles and are measured in inches, generally going in 2 in intervals. Leather ones are the most expensive but if properly cared for will give long lasting service. They are good for fit horses but may cause galling on horses in soft condition.

The three-fold girth is a piece of leather folded in three and is used with the fold to the front ie behind the horse's elbow. If the edge were to the front then rubbing could occur. These girths must be made from substantial leather so the folds form a soft roll and not a crease. A piece of oiled cloth should be kept inside the girth to ensure the leather stays supple.

Balding and Atherstone leather girths are shaped to fit behind the horse's elbows whilst avoiding any rubbing or soreness. The Balding differs from the Atherstone in that the leather is split into three and plaited over to gain the shaping whilst the Atherstone is one continuous piece of shaped leather.

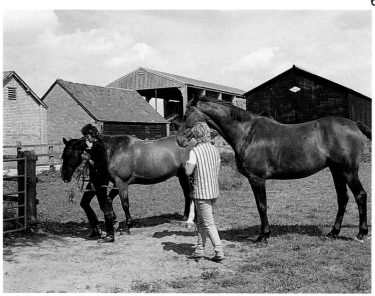

Above *When turning horses out, always face them towards the gate — this protects you from flying hooves if the horses suddenly take off to enjoy their freedom.*

Below *You scratch my back . . . These two friends can spend as much as an hour 'grooming' each other.*

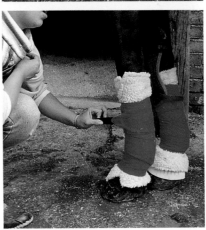

Always apply bandages over padding which extends from below the knee or hock to the coronet. Start just below the knee or hock, leaving the first couple of inches of bandage at an angle to the leg. Make one turn with the bandage, then fold down the angled piece of bandage and make another turn to cover the flap. Continue bandaging down the leg, ensuring that the pressure is even all the way down. As you reach the coronet the bandage will take a natural turn upwards. Continue until you reach your starting point again — if the bandage is short you may only reach the mid-way point. Secure the velcro or tapes, remembering that tapes must not be tied on the front or back of the leg. Tuck any tape ends away under the bandage for safety.

To fit strapless overreach boots, turn them inside out, then they can be pulled over the hoof. If this proves difficult, pieces of baler twine threaded through the boot make it easier to pull them on. Once on, the boots are then turned the right way. Using overreach boots for travelling will offer protection against the horse treading on himself during the journey.

Tail bandaging — unroll a few inches of bandage, place this under the tail and make one turn with the bandage as securely as you can.

Fold down the spare piece of bandage and secure it by making another turn of the bandage. If you make this turn above the first, it will give added security.

Bandage down the tail, making even and neat turns, with the pressure constant throughout.

The bandage should be long enough to allow you to bandage along the length of the tail bone and then back up again to the half-way point. Secure the tapes and tuck any spare ends in neatly. Complete your bandaging by bending the tail gently back into shape.

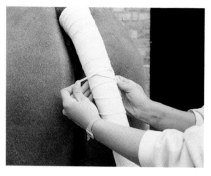

Above *Three types of saddle. From left to right: a jumping saddle, with the forward cut flaps; a dressage saddle showing the straighter flap and longer girth straps (these saddles are as bulk free as possible to ensure closer contact for the rider); and a general-purpose saddle.*

Below *Saddles need to fit both horse and rider — this saddle is too small for this particular horse. It's a general-purpose saddle intended for a 14.2hh pony, not a 16hh horse.*

Above One way of bridling — by passing your right hand under the horse's jaw and on to his nose you can hold his head steady whilst your left hand helps to guide the bit into place. NB: The horse is secured to an outside tying-up ring via his headcollar which has been placed around his neck whilst the bridle is fitted.

Below Another way of bridling. In this picture you can see how the thumb is used to encourage the horse to open his mouth and accept the bit.

Above *When putting on any rug fold it in half and place it well up the horse's neck. Then fold it down and pull it gently into place, so ensuring that the horse's coat lies flat. If your rug requires a roller then you should secure the rug with this before doing up any leg or breast straps.*

Below *A well-fitting stable rug — it is darted to give a snug fit around the quarters, has cross surcingles so keeping it in place without exerting any pressure on the spine, and has plenty of depth.*

Above *Tacked up and ready to ride — note the numnah showing all round the saddle.*

Below *Occasionally riding out in poor light cannot be avoided — exercise sheets such as this fluorescent example will ensure that motorists see you. Stirrup lights and fluorescent strips on the horse's tail and back legs are also sensible precautions.*

String girths are made from strings of nylon and are relatively cheap and strong. However, you must take care to ensure that folds of the horse's skin are not trapped between the strings. Sweat can cause the strings to become hard but the girths are easy to wash.

Cotton-covered girths with a spongy padding such as the Cottage Craft one are sensibly priced and hard wearing. They are soft but strong and are easily washed. Lampwick girths are soft, strong and good for use on horses in soft condition.

Numnahs are saddle-shaped pieces of cloth — they can be made in sheepskin, felt, simulated sheepskin, nylon and cotton-covered foam. They are attached to the saddle by tapes or loops and a correctly fitted numnah would be pulled up well into the front arch and show about 1 in (2.5cm) all round under the saddle.

Numnahs should not really be necessary if your saddle fits well but people often use them to protect the horse's back if riding for long periods in a spring-tree saddle, because these saddles tend to concentrate pressure on to a limited area. In addition, numnahs help keep the saddle lining clean. They can also be used to protect a horse's back when jumping, since as the horse arches his back over a fence it is possible that his spine could touch the gullet of the saddle. They are also useful with sensitive and cold-backed horses.

Bridles

These come in pony, cob and full size and are usually supplied with reins and noseband but without a bit. The width of the leatherwork varies according to the bridle's intended use; for example show bridles have thin, perhaps rolled leatherwork, whereas a hunting bridle has broader leather.

New leather will stretch so you may have to alter the fitting of your bridle accordingly. It is now possible to buy webbing bridles which are much easier to clean, but the overall appearance is not as impressive as leather.

Nosebands

There is a wide choice of nosebands, all with specific purposes. Cavesson nosebands are plain nosebands used to complete bridles. If you wish to use a standing martingale you would attach it to either a cavesson or a flash noseband. The latter is a strong cavesson but with an additional, detachable strap attached to the centre of the nosepiece which fastens below the bit in the curb groove. This helps to prevent the horse evading the bit by opening his mouth and crossing the jaw.

Dropped nosebands also keep the horse's mouth shut so he cannot put any evasions into practice. This noseband also produces pressure on the horse's nose, and when used with a snaffle bit, strengthens the action of the bit and helps to position the horse's head correctly.

Grakle nosebands have two straps and resemble a figure of eight. Both straps are buckled behind the jaw bone with one fastening above the bit and the other below. Pressure is applied to the nose where the two straps intersect at the front.

You can find out from your horse's previous owner which noseband the horse is used to wearing. It is also worth consulting with your instructor before changing your horse's tack around. All items of tack are expensive and there is no point buying a grakle just because it is fashionable if your horse does not need to wear one.

Reins

Plain leather reins may be supplied with a bridle; these are fine except that they become slippery and difficult to hold when it is raining or they have become wet due to a sweaty horse. Laced and plaited leather reins are also available, of which plaited give a better grip.

Rubber-covered reins are very popular as they give good grip in all kinds of conditions. Continental reins are made from web with pieces of leather acting as grips placed at even distances along the rein length. However, they are not as easy to keep clean as rubber reins.

Bits

A bit, in conjunction with other parts of the bridle, will act on certain pressure points on the horse's head and mouth. Different bits act on different combinations of these points, dependent upon their type, fit and action. The pressure points are the lips, bars, corners and roof of the horse's mouth, the tongue, the chin-groove, nose and poll.

As this is your first horse, hopefully you will have an animal who goes kindly in a snaffle bit. In this group of bits the mouthpieces may be jointed or mullen-mouthed (half-moon shape) and the rings may be fixed or loose. The mild action of the mullen-mouthed snaffle puts even pressure across the horse's tongue and bars of the mouth whilst the jointed snaffle has a nutcracker action, acting more on the tongue and corners of the mouth than on the bars. The bits may be made of rubber, vulcanite or metal.

Double-jointed snaffle bits may also be found. For instance the French bradoon has a spatula in the middle of the mouthpiece which reduces the nutcracker action and lessens the risk of the tongue being caught in the joint. Do not confuse this bit with the much severer Dr Bristol snaffle where the double joint is formed by a square plate which presses into the tongue when pressure is applied to the reins.

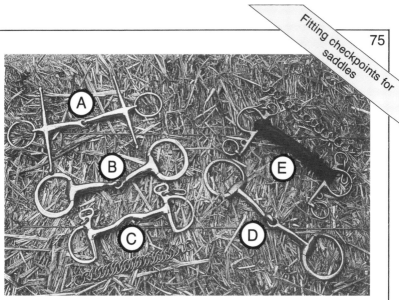

A = Fulmer snaffle; B = German snaffle; C = Kimblewick and curb chain; D = Snaffle which is made of nickel; E = Rubber pelham (note the worn pieces on the mouthpiece).

Fitting checkpoints for saddles

1 If you are buying from a saddler then you should be able to visit them or vice versa in order to try a variety of saddles on the horse. With their expert advice the result should be a saddle which fits both the horse and the rider.

2 Unless you intend to specialize in showjumping, dressage etc, then it is likely you will be buying a general-purpose saddle.

3 The size of the saddle is given in inches and the measurement represents the length of the seat. The normal range of sizes is 12 to 18 in.

4 A saddle must not place any pressure on the horse's loins or spine. The weight of the saddle should be evenly distributed over the lumbar muscles which cover the upper part of the ribs.

5 There should be a clear channel along the horse's spine, so the gullet of the saddle needs to be wide enough to stop the panels bearing on the spine. With the rider on board you should be able to see along the whole length of the saddle — check from both the front and back. Remember that a new saddle will bed down so allow for this when checking clearance of the spine.

6 Check that the saddle sits level on the horse's back. The weight of the rider should be evenly distributed across the whole bearing surface. If the saddle panels are incorrectly stuffed then undue pressure or friction on the horse's back will result.

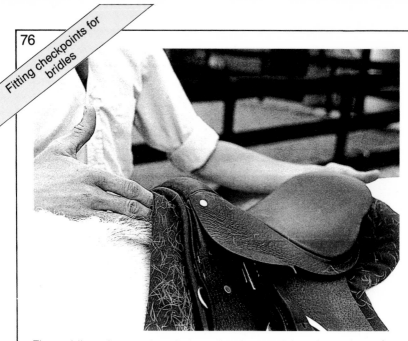

The saddle arch must clear the pony's withers and there has to be a clear channel between the pony's back and the saddle.

7 Look at the saddle in relation to the horse's withers. It should not pinch nor bear down on them. Different widths of saddle are available to cater for the variations in equine frames. The saddle should give sufficient clearance of the withers; when mounted you should be able to slip three fingers between the saddle arch and withers.

8 Check that the panels of the saddle are not hampering the movement of the horse's shoulders.

9 When the rider is mounted and sitting correctly, test that the saddle is large enough for the rider. There should be room for the width of the rider's palm between the rider's bottom and the saddle cantle.

Fitting checkpoints for bridles

1 You should be able to insert a hand's width between the throatlash and the horse's cheekbone. If you fit the throatlash too tightly you will be restricting the horse's flexion at the poll and interfering with his breathing.

2 The browband stops the bridle from slipping backwards up the horse's neck, but it must not be fitted too tightly or it will irritate and rub the horse. You should be able to fit two fingers behind it.

3 Cavesson nosebands should be fitted so that they lie half-way between the projecting cheekbones and the corners of the mouth.

Another test for fitting is for the noseband to lie two fingers' width below the projecting cheekbone. As far as tightness is concerned you need to be able to slip two fingers between the horse's nose and the noseband.

4 Drop nosebands need to be carefully fitted so that they do not interfere with the horse's breathing. All too often they are fitted far too low. The front of the noseband needs to be well above the nostrils so it does not hamper the air flow. The back of the noseband sits in the chin groove. It should be tight enough to prevent the horse from crossing his jaw.

5 The bit should be high enough in the mouth so that the horse 'smiles', ie, the corners of his mouth are slightly wrinkled. If the bit is too high the horse will look uncomfortable; if too low the bit may bang on the horse's teeth.

6 It is important that the bit is of the correct width for the horse's mouth. Too narrow and it will pinch the horse; too wide and it will slide about causing bruising and discomfort. To check the width hold the bit in the horse's mouth so that the mouthpiece is straight. There should be about ¼ in clearance on either side.

7 Ensure that the cheek pieces, which together with the headpiece hold the bit in the horse's mouth, are of the same length and are adjusted to the same hole on each side.

8 Make sure all the straps are home in their keepers and that nothing is twisted.

9 Bits are measured in inches, the measurement being taken when the bit is lying flat. The mouthpiece, excluding the rings, is measured.

10 Martingales should fit with enough room to admit a hand's width between the horse's withers and the neckstrap. The buckle of the neckstrap lies on the nearside. When a running martingale is attached to the girth, the two rings should reach to the horse's throat to ensure a good fit. When a standing martingale is fitted there should be enough strap at the front to hold up into the horse's jaw. If it is too tight then the movement of the horse's head and neck will be restricted which could also affect the horse's balance.

Cleaning and caring for tack

As your tack has been a major investment it is wise to protect it by looking after all your equipment properly. Apart from making sense financially such an attitude will also help your horse, because he will appreciate having clean, supple tack — hard, uncared for equipment will gall his skin and be uncomfortable to wear — and you, because every time you clean your tack you can check it over for safety and attend to any repairs.

Ideally your tack should be cleaned after each ride but in practice this is difficult, especially if you have a job, house and family to keep

All billets and buckles need regular safety checks. Look carefully for cracks where the leather is bent over, and remember to give these areas particular attention when you are cleaning your tack.

happy as well as your horse! However, you must always wash the bit after you have ridden. If you don't your poor horse will have to put up with something akin to you eating your tea off a dirty plate!

If time allows, it is worth giving your tack a quick wipe over after each ride. In any case, make sure you set aside one session per week for thorough tack cleaning. By this I mean taking your saddle and bridle to pieces so you can give them a really good clean. Here's how.

You will need a bucket of warm water, sponges, an old towel, saddle soap, neatsfoot oil and cloth, and a roll of horse hair; after you have pulled your horse's mane or tail keep some of the hairs to form a ball for tack cleaning.

Strip your saddle by removing the numnah, stirrup irons and leathers, girth and girth guards. Take your bridle to pieces as well, remembering to take notice by which hole the cheek pieces are attached to the head piece and on which hole the noseband is fastened.

Place the bit and stirrup irons in the water. Wet one of your sponges, squeeze it out until it is just damp and systemically wipe over all your leather work, removing all the grease and dirt. Use the rolled up ball of horse hair to remove stubborn grease spots. Avoid getting your leather too wet. Clean both sides of the leather, paying particular attention to where the leather folds over. Always use this time to check the stitching on your tack. It is better to spot any problem early and attend to it to avoid any accidents.

Now turn to the metal work. Wipe the irons and bit clean with your towel. You should make regular checks to ascertain whether the bit is becoming worn.

Place these to one side while you saddle soap the leather. Using a slightly damp sponge, rub it across a bar of saddle soap. Then, using a circular motion, soap all the leather work. If you are producing a lather then your sponge is too damp — you want the leather work to receive the maximum benefit from the soap and this is not achieved if the soap lathers. Remember to soap both sides of the leather.

Re-assemble your tack and 'put it up' for storage as follows. Attach the irons and leathers to the saddle. Do not attach the girth to the girth straps, but instead lie it across the seat of the saddle, with the girth ends slipped through the stirrup irons. Place the numnah on top of the saddle with the underside facing up so that the air can get to it. (Numnahs should be brushed over when you clean your tack and washed thoroughly when the need arises. Most can be washed by machine. Do not let your numnah become hard through dirt and dried sweat.) For the bridle, thread the reins and martingale through the throatlash and then fasten the throatlash. Undo the noseband, wrap it around all the bridle and then loosely thread the noseband strap through its keeper to ensure everything stays together.

Every so often you may need to oil your tack. For instance, the lower strap of a grakle noseband can start to become hard as it is often wetted by the horse's saliva. It may therefore need to be oiled every two to three weeks in order to retain its suppleness, in addition to your normal tack cleaning procedure.

Other pieces of tack are not likely to need such regular oiling but it's worth having an 'oiling session' every few months or so. Use a soft cloth to apply a little oil at a time, using a circular action to rub the oil into the leather. Beware of applying too much and making the leather over greasy.

If for any reason you need to store tack for a while, clean it as normal and then apply a thin layer of petroleum jelly to the leather. Should you find that mould has developed on your tack, remove it using a dry cloth, then sterilize the leather with one of the materials available from babycare counters. Then clean your tack as normal.

Other leather items such as brushing boots, headcollars, strappings on rugs, knee and hock boots etc also need regular care. Boots made from synthetic materials can usually be washed in a machine, but check the manufacturer's advice first.

Equipment for your horse

There is an abundance of horse equipment. Just walk into any saddler's and you will be confronted by boots, bandages, rugs and so on in a whole wealth of styles, materials and colours. For a new owner such a wide range can present problems. Can you distinguish between a brushing boot and a tendon boot? Which rugs does your horse really need? How do you know which size rug to buy for your horse?

Let's take a look at some of this equipment.

Boots

Brushing boots Brushing usually occurs in the fetlock area, where the horse strikes into himself with the opposite limb. This may be because the horse's conformation and action predisposes him to brushing, or he may be tired and overworked and so knocks himself. Horses which are weak, underfed, young and green, unbalanced, or wearing heavy, poorly-fitting shoes, may also brush.

Brushing boots protect the horse's legs in the area where brushing (also known as an interfering injury) takes place. The boots may be made of leather, felt or synthetic materials and can be used on all four legs. The boots have a reinforced pad which runs the length of the boot and is larger in the fetlock area. Generally five-strap boots are used on the hind legs whilst three and four-strap boots are used on the forelegs.

As brushing injuries can occur easily, these boots are a wise investment. They are quickly fitted and are a sensible precaution when jumping or schooling your horse. Some owners like to fit protective boots on their horse whenever they ride, even though the horse may not actually brush. It is a case of 'a stitch in time'.

Before you fit boots, always check that there is no mud on the

Boots galore — a is a tendon boot; b, c, d and e are all brushing boots; f and g are knee caps; and f is what is known as a skeleton knee cap.

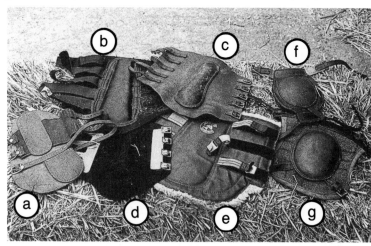

Right Brushing boots fitted on to the forelegs — you can see the padded area of the boot which protects the fetlock and the area immediately above.

Below Another type of brushing boot — sheepskin lined with elasticated, 'velcro' straps . . .

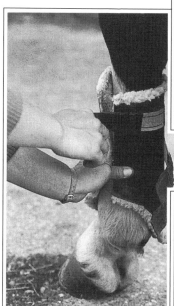

Right . . . and elasticated straps which hook neatly across the 'velcro' straps for extra security.

underside which can rub a horse's legs. Place them around the cannon bone, well above the fetlock joint and then slide the boot into position. Fasten the straps securely, not so tight as to restrict circulation, but not so loose that the boot slips down and creates a potential hazard. Make sure that you keep the pressure even all the way down the boot. These boots are fitted on the correct leg if the straps point backwards. When you remove any boot or bandage always massage the horse's legs to help his circulation.

Whilst protective boots are sensible in most instances there is an exception. If you go hunting it is worth considering leaving the boots off, especially if the conditions are likely to be bad. Bits of dirt and stones can work their way between the boot and your horse's leg, so causing a nasty rub or sore if you are out all day. If, however, you are only out for a couple of hours and the going is dry you may wish to use boots.

Tendon boots These are used on the front legs only and protect the tendons of the horse's forelegs from injury, from, for example, a high over-reach, when galloping or jumping.

Tendon boots are padded to give protection against injury and they also offer support for the legs. They are shaped to fit the back of the leg whilst the straps are fastened around the front of the leg, again with the straps pointing backwards.

Fetlock boots These are a type of brushing boot but they are smaller, covering only the fetlock area. They may have only one or two straps.

Yorkshire boots These serve the same purpose as the fetlock boots, but they are generally only made from felt. Tapes are used to secure them rather than straps.

Over-reach boots Easily recognizable by their bell shape, these boots are fitted over the horse's front hooves to protect against over-reach injuries. These occur when the toe of the horse's hind shoe catches the fore foot, usually in the heel region, for example when galloping or jumping in heavy going.

Over-reach boots can be bought either with or without straps. Those with straps are easier to put on although some people feel that such boots are also prone to coming off easily, particularly when you don't want them to! Having used both types, I find they can both come off in the middle of a cross-country round; it is a matter of personal preference.

Another use for these boots is for wear during journeys. Some horses have a tendency to tread on themselves whilst travelling and over-reach boots, fitted on all four feet, provide protection for the coronary band.

These boots should be fitted fairly tightly so that they do not revolve around the foot. To fit the strapless boots, turn them inside out and pull them over the hoof, as illustrated on page 67.

Knee caps There are two types of knee caps, skeleton caps and the fuller ones. Knee caps may be used to protect a horse when travelling, or during exercise. If, for instance, the roads in your area are slippery or you have to ride out in slippery conditions, knee caps will protect against broken knees if your horse goes down. If you are riding a young or inexperienced horse over fixed fences then knee caps are a sensible measure.

The top strap of a knee cap should be firmly fastened while the lower one needs to be looser to allow for movement of the horse's knee. All the straps fasten on the outside of the leg, with the straps pointing backwards.

Hock boots These are generally used to protect a horse's hocks from knocks; for example, during travelling some animals tend to lean against the trailer ramp. The same principles apply to the fitting of the straps on these boots as with the knee caps.

Travelling boots Whatever the length of journey it makes sense to protect your horse's legs whilst he is travelling. There is now a whole range of boots on the market for travelling. Some simply cover the lower leg whilst others incorporate knee and hock protection as well. Whilst travelling boots offer adequate protection, bandages will give more support if the horse has to undertake a long journey.

Bandages

Stable/travelling bandages One set of bandages doubles for use in the stable and when travelling. These bandages are usually about 4 in (10cm) wide and 7 or 8 ft (2.1 or 2.4m) in length. They used to be made from a woollen mixture, but now a wider range of materials is used, including stockinette.

Whatever purpose they are used for, these bandages must be applied over gamgee or some other suitable padding. The gamgee (cotton wool between open-weave gauze) is wrapped around the horse's leg taking care to cover the vulnerable coronary band. Start just below the knee or hock, leaving a couple of inches of bandage free, as in the picture on page 66. Pass the bandage around the leg for one turn, then fold down the overlap as shown. Continue to bandage down the leg to the coronet when the bandage can then take a natural turn upwards. You should be able to carry on bandaging and finish at your starting place. Tie the tapes, tuck in the ends and fold a piece of bandage over them.

It is important to keep the pressure even all the way down the bandage, because if the bandage is tighter in some places than others it can cause damage to the tendons. Ringed marks or lumps on a horse's legs are indications of such damage. The tapes should not be tied tighter than the rest of the bandage or swellings can occur. Always tie the tapes on the outside or inside of the leg, never at the front of the leg on the bone or at the back of the leg on the tendon.

Bandages should not be left on for periods of more than 12

hours at a time. Remove them and reapply the bandage at regular intervals.

When re-rolling bandages the tapes should be on the inside.

Exercise/support bandages You may have noticed that some riders prefer to use exercise/support bandages rather than protective boots. Provided they are fitted correctly they can serve a useful purpose, but if they are used incorrectly they can cause damage. For instance some people insist on using exercise bandages without any protective gamgee underneath; you should *never* do this! These bandages are elasticated and so they can tighten on the horse's legs when wet, so restricting the circulation. Horses who have suffered from such owners have tell-tale marks on their legs.

Exercise/support bandages are used when the horse is working for protection against injury, to support tendons and reinforce weak tendons, but do not use them unless they are necessary, or you can find that your horse comes to depend upon them. They also have veterinary uses as pressure bandages, for example to help disperse swellings.

These bandages differ from stable bandages as they are only 2-3 in (5-7.5cm) wide and are usually made from crepe or stockinette. They are fitted from just below the knee to just above the fetlock. It is wise to stitch the tapes together or secure with adhesive if you use these bandages for protection when riding across country etc, because a bandage which becomes untied could cause problems.

When removing any bandages do not try to roll them up as you remove them, but hang them up to air first.

Tail bandages These are similar in appearance to the exercise bandages and are used to improve the tail's appearance and protect the tail against injury when travelling. In common with other bandages they must not be left on for long periods, and *never* leave the tail bandage on overnight.

Damp the hairs of the tail before applying the bandage so that they lie flat. Never damp the bandage as it may shrink whilst on the tail causing injury. The picture sequence on page 68 shows how to bandage a tail. Remember to keep the pressure even throughout. Bend the bandaged tail gently back into position. When you wish to remove the bandage undo the tapes and then, taking hold of the bandage at the top, gently slide it downwards and off. If you have applied a bandage over a plaited tail you need to unroll the bandage to remove it in order not to spoil the tail plait.

Rugs

Stable rugs These are used for:
1. Clipped horses who need a replacement for their lost coats.
2. Thin-skinned horses who require extra warmth in colder periods.
3. Sick animals who may need extra warmth.

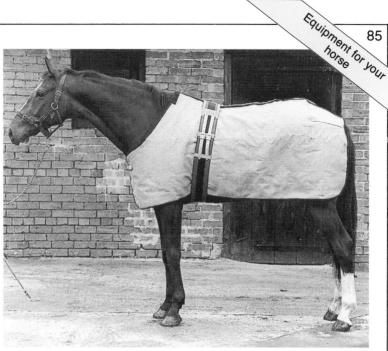

For your horse's rug measurement you need to know the length from the centre of the horse's chest, around the shoulder and along his side to an imaginary vertical line down from the horse's dock. Measure your horse's depth too — from his withers to about 4 inches below the elbow. Some rugs are rather short so if you know the depth your horse requires you can look for rugs which are more generously cut.

4. Any animal requiring extra warmth during cold weather.

Stable rugs come in a variety of materials, styles and prices. Jute rugs were the traditional ones, but now there is plenty of choice in the quilted rug range, rather like the continental quilt development over recent years for human bedding. Some rugs, like jute ones, need rollers which are bought separately, in order to keep the rug and any underblankets in place, whilst other rugs have surcingles as an integral part of the rug.

New Zealand rugs These are used for protection against the wind, rain and cold in late autumn and winter for horses who are living out and for stabled horses when they are turned out to graze. They are made from waterproof canvas with a woollen mixture lining and legstraps. Some rugs have integral surcingles. Recent developments have introduced other, lighter materials to the traditional canvas. Another recent addition to some designs has been a flap which covers the top of the horse's tail so giving extra protection.

In common with other rugs, New Zealands come in different weight

Above *If your horse needs to wear a blanket under his rug, fold the front of the blanket back as shown before putting the rug on.*

Below *The spare end of the blanket can then be folded back and secured under the roller. An extra piece of foam under the roller would be a sensible precaution against pressure on the spine.*

Summer sheets are generally made of cotton — note the sponge under the roller to keep undue pressure off the horse's spine.

qualities, and the better the canvas quality the more hardwearing it is likely to be. There are some very cheap rugs on the market and you have to be wary of the ones which are neither substantial nor well-designed.

If your horse lives out you will need two New Zealand rugs so that if one is absolutely soaked he can still be kept dry and warm whilst the other rug is drying out.

Day rugs Usually made of woollen material and generally used now for transporting to or wearing at shows for a smart appearance. At one time, day rugs were used in the stable during the day whilst the stable rugs were reserved for night-time wear. However, most owners now use the stable rug throughout the day, adding extra rugs or blankets at night depending on weather conditions.

Many day rugs carry the owner's initials or the horse's name on the corner of the rug. The rugs are available in a variety of colours and usually have matching or contrasting binding.

HORSE CARE

Grooming

One of the everyday jobs of horse ownership is grooming, but there is more to this work than simply making the horse look good. Regular grooming stimulates the horse's circulation, removes waste products, tones up his muscles, improves the coat condition and helps to prevent disease, especially of the skin. In addition, grooming removes grease and scurf from the horse's coat, so ensuring cleanliness.

Daily grooming also provides an opportunity for an owner to check the horse over for any cuts, knocks, swellings or areas of heat. Most horses enjoy the massage effect of being groomed, and it is a good

Grooming is one of the many jobs you can help with, either at your local riding school or assisting a private owner, and it is all good practice in case you decide to have a go at horsey exams.

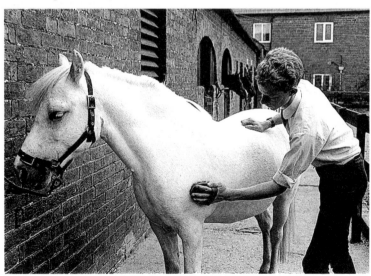

way of accustoming youngsters to being handled.

There are different types of grooming, and the conditions under which a horse is kept will dictate the amount of grooming he receives. For instance, horses who have to live out all year will need the grease and oils in their coats as protection against the elements. It is therefore unfair to give such horses a thorough daily grooming which removes the vital grease from their coats.

Horses living out can roll or scratch at leisure so stimulating their own glands whereas a stabled horse relies on you to do the job for him through grooming.

Grooming can be split into quartering, strapping and setting fair. Quartering is the name given to the attention a horse receives before exercise, in which he is brushed over where his tack will fit, his feet are picked out, his eyes sponged and he is generally made presentable and comfortable. This process will usually take five to ten minutes.

Strapping is a much more thorough process, usually taking about three-quarters of an hour, and is generally done after exercise. One method of strapping is described later (page 91).

Setting fair is done before the horse is left for the night. Again it is a fairly quick process, with the horse being brushed over, feet picked out, and then eyes, nose and dock (the area under the tail) sponged.

The grooming kit

This consists of several items, all with specific uses and names.

Dandy brush This has long, stiff bristles and is particularly useful for removing heavy mud and dirt, but should not be used on a horse's head or his mane and tail as they can cause the hairs to split.

These brushes are used more on grass-kept animals, because they do not remove the oil and grease from the coat to the same extent as body brushes. Dandy brushes can be used with a to and fro motion on horses with reasonably thick coats, which makes it easier to remove caked mud. If dandy brushes are used on thin-skinned or recently clipped horses, they should be used gently and sparingly.

Body brush These brushes have much smaller, softer and close-set bristles which reach down to the roots of the horse's coat, removing grease, dust and scurf. Body brushes can be used on the more sensitive parts of the horse, ie his head, belly region, and on the mane and tail. The brush is used with short, circular strokes in the direction of the coat hair. Hold the brush in your right hand if you are grooming the right hand side of the horse. After every six strokes or so the body brush is cleaned using a curry comb. Metal curry combs are the best for this job — knock the comb on the floor or wall regularly to remove the collected scurf.

Curry comb Rubber curry combs are used to remove mud and dirt from heavy-coated horses and are often more efficient than dandy brushes. If your horse is moulting, a rubber curry comb is good for

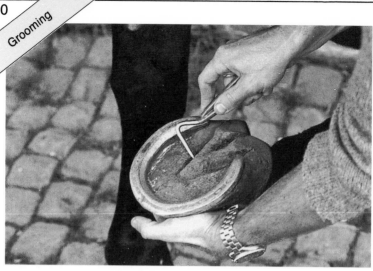

Do not use a hoofpick in this way as you could damage the frog (the V-shaped cleft). Always use the pick from the heel to toe.

removing loose hair. Used with a gentle, circular motion, they have a massage effect. Never use curry combs on bony parts of a horse, ie head or legs.

Plastic curry combs are also available. These have longer spikes than the rubber comb and should not be used on thin-skinned horses.

Water brush This soft-bristled brush is used to damp the mane and tail, to remove sweatmarks or to clean the horse's feet.

Hoofpick Used for removing stones, packed earth and mud from the underside of the horse's feet.

Hoof oil This helps to improve the appearance of the feet and is also good for brittle feet.

Sponges You will need at least two sponges: one to clean the horse's eyes and nose and the other for cleaning the dock.

Mane and tail comb Usually made of metal, this can be used to help untangle a mane or tail, but is generally used for pulling.

Massage pad/wisp These are used to tone up the muscles on the side of the horse's neck, quarters and thighs. Wisps are plaited ropes of hay or straw while massage pads are generally made from leather. They are banged down in the direction of the coat, the number of times a horse is wisped depending upon the required fitness level. Neither wisps nor pads should be used on the tender loin region or on bony parts.

Cactus cloth This is not an essential piece of kit, but is useful for removing stable or grass stains and sweat marks. Made from an open weave sacking type material.

Sweat scraper This is a long flexible blade of smooth metal or rubber which is used to remove excess sweat or water from the coat after washing. It is used gently but firmly in the direction of the hair; be very careful and use the rubber variety for the bony parts, and do not use at all below the knees or hocks.

Tail bandage Made from stockinette or crepe, this is used to improve the appearance of the tail. Must not be left on overnight!

Stable rubber Rather like a linen teacloth, this is used damp to give the horse a final wipe-over and polish after grooming.

Grooming gloves These are useful for removing loose hair when the horse is changing his coat. Made from pimpled rubber, they can also be used for massage.

Kit tray A heavy-duty plastic tray with a carrying handle is needed to keep your kit together, clean and tidy.

Care of your grooming kit

Infections can be spread by brushes so try to keep your kit for your horse's exclusive use. Give all your brushes a regular clean in warm soapy water, but do not immerse the whole brush or the wood will be damaged. Use your fingers to clean the brush bristles and make sure they are thoroughly rinsed. Give them a final rinse in a saline solution to harden the bristles.

Stable rubbers and some sponges can be boiled to clean them. If any of your brushes are leather backed, make sure you keep the leather supple.

How to groom

The thorough grooming process known as strapping is preferably done after exercise as the horse's pores are then open, the skin is warm and dust and scurf are at the surface. Carrying out this procedure properly will require considerable effort from you and no doubt at first you will find it quite a tiring task!

Make sure you have all your grooming equipment plus a bucket of water and a headcollar and rope. If it is a sunny day, it can be pleasant grooming your horse outside, but tie him up safely. Whenever you tie up a horse make sure the leadrope is tied through a piece of breakable string rather than on to a fixed object. This will ensure that if the horse panics for any reason and pulls back the string will break. If the horse is tied to a solid object such as a ring in the stable wall, he could cause himself considerable damage.

For safety's sake, never stand directly behind a horse, but always keep to one side. Remember to speak to your horse, especially before you move around his hindquarters. It is easy to startle a horse and his reaction could well be to kick out. Think and act with safety in mind.

First of all, remove any sweat marks or mud from the horse, using a dandy brush or rubber curry comb. Pay particular attention to the

The safest way of clipping a lead rope on to a headcollar.

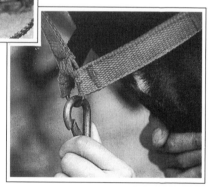

areas where the horse's tack has been in contact with his body and to the belly. The dandy brush can be held in either hand and should be used with a to and fro motion.

Always wear sensible footwear around horses — flimsy sandals are dangerous.

As you work around the horse, be careful that you do not kneel or sit near him, but squat or bend down when attending to the lower legs. If you kneel down, your horse could easily injure you if anything caused him to jump to the side. When working on the hind legs it is sensible to take hold of your horse's tail and hold it to one side. This discourages a horse from kicking out, something a ticklish animal may be prone to do. It also prevents the horse from swishing his tail in your face.

Once the mud is off, it is time to set to work with the body brush. (Remember that this part of grooming is best left out of the routine for a grass-kept horse.) Start work on the near side, with the body brush in the left hand and metal curry comb in the right. You need to lean your weight behind each stroke of the brush, so stand back from the horse, keep your arm slightly bent and your wrist supple. Use the brush in short circular strokes with the lay of the coat, cleaning the brush after every few strokes with the curry comb. Use the curry comb away from your wrist so that you do not accidentally injure yourself.

Swap sides but before you start grooming on the offside push the mane over to the other side so that you can groom the crest thoroughly. Once you have finished with the horse's body you can turn your attention to the mane. This takes some time as you need to deal with a few locks of hair at a time, separating the tangles with your fingers, brushing the hairs and then the roots.

To groom the horse's head, remove the headcollar and fasten it temporarily around his neck. You will only need the body brush so your free hand can be used to steady the horse's head. Be gentle with the brush, taking extra care around the eyes. As soon as you've completed the head, replace the headcollar.

Now deal with the horse's tail. It is often quicker to use your fingers to separate any tangles, working up from the bottom of the tail to the roots. Avoid pulling out hairs. Some horses have such fine tails that brushing removes too many hairs and the only way to keep the tails tangle free is for the owner to separate the locks using fingers.

You can now use a wisp or massage pad. The time spent on this part of grooming will vary according to the level of muscle tone your horse requires for the work he does. Both sides of the horse should receive the same amount of wisping, which should be built up gradually.

Take one of your sponges, and wring it out in warm water so it is soft and clean. Attend to the eyes first, working away from the corners and around the eyelids. Wring out the sponge again before using it on the muzzle region, sponging the lips, inside and outside of the nostrils. Use a separate sponge for the dock region, lifting the tail as high as possible and sponging the skin on the underside of the tail. Most horses find this very refreshing.

You may wish to apply a tail bandage to help improve the appearance of your horse's tail. Always dampen the tail hairs, never the bandage itself or it could shrink and tighten while on the tail. See picture sequence on page 68 for the method of tail bandaging. It is vital that you do not leave the tail bandage on for too long, and certainly not overnight. There have been instances of horses losing their tails because bandages have been applied too tightly and left on too long.

Damp the bristles of the water brush and then brush down from the

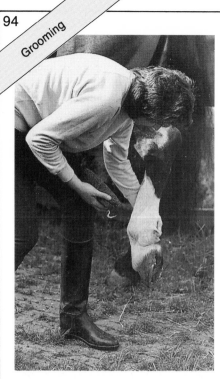

Picking up a hind foot — note that the owner has run her hand along the inside of the horse's leg so that even if the horse were to kick out he would not injure her arm.

roots of the horse's mane so that his mane is 'laid'. A horse's mane is meant to lie on the offside of the neck, so if your horse's mane tries to misbehave you can lay the mane or plait it to 'train' it to lie on the correct side.

Using the hoofpick from the heel to the toe, clean out the horse's feet. Pick up each foot in turn, always working in the same order so that your horse will soon learn the routine and be ready to lift his foot. To pick up a forefoot run your hand down the back of the horse's leg, push gently against him so that his weight is shifted on to the other foot and lift up the leg. You may need to squeeze the base of the tendon gently if the horse is resistant to picking up his feet. Support his hoof in your hand. With the hind legs you need to run your hand down the inside of the leg. Whichever foot you are picking up, you should be facing the rear of the horse. Do not place your arm behind a horse's hind leg because if he were to kick out your arm could easily be broken.

The hoofpick is used from heel to toe so that there is no risk of the pick going into the soft parts of the horse's frog. Make sure the cleft of the frog is free from dirt. Use this opportunity to check the condition of your horse's shoes. Tap each to see if it is secure, check if any shoes are wearing thin and run your fingers around the clenches to feel if any have risen.

You can save time and effort by picking out the horse's feet into a skip rather than dirtying the bedding or stable yard. Sometimes you may need to wash the mud off your horse's feet. Use the water brush and keep your thumb pressed into the hollow of the horse's heel to prevent water getting into this area where the skin is often sensitive. If the weather is cold it is best to leave washing the feet.

Hoof oil can then be applied with a small paint brush. Lift up the feet and apply oil over the sole, frog and bulbs of the heels. Then with the foot on the floor, apply oil to the coronary band and over the wall of the foot.

To complete the process damp the stable rubber and go all over the horse to remove any traces of dust.

In colder weather you can groom without completely removing the horse's rugs. Just fold back the rugs from the front, groom as necessary, replace the rugs, fold back the rugs from the rear and groom. When you have finished make sure all the rugs are comfortably in place.

Shoeing

One of the most famous and apt sayings of the horse world is 'no foot, no horse'. Your horse's feet need regular and *expert* attention and if you fail to provide this then your horse will suffer, and you will have nothing to ride.

Irrespective of whether your horse wears shoes or not, whether he is ridden or not, whether he is young or old, he needs attention from a farrier every six to eight weeks. In fact, the interval between visits may be shorter; for instance horses used for long-distance riding tend to wear their shoes out quicker.

You will find your local farrier in the Yellow Pages, by writing to the Worshipful Company of Farriers, or by asking your local riding school, club or livery yard to recommend one.

Farriers tend to be busy particularly if they are good and therefore in demand by the local horsey community. So give plenty of notice that your horse requires a visit. You cannot expect to ring the farrier one day and have him attending to your horse the next.

Once you have found a good farrier and you know your horse's requirements you can book your visits every five weeks or so. If this is not feasible then make a note in your diary two or three weeks after your farrier's visit to telephone him and fix the next appointment. Once you have fixed a time for a visit make sure you or your representative is there to hold the horse. Your farrier will not appreciate arriving at a field to shoe a horse only to find that he is expected to catch the animal first and then turn the horse out again once the job is over! If the weather is bad it is helpful to have somewhere under cover where the farrier can work.

A good farrier can be an excellent friend to a new owner, and if you take the opportunity to talk to your farrier you will learn a great deal about caring for your horse's feet. Establish a relationship and it will pay dividends later; for instance if your horse casts a shoe just before a show and needs urgent attention!

Types of shoeing

Hot shoeing Shoes are made on the spot to the individual horse's requirements so you may have to take the horse along to the farrier's forge. Some farriers have a travelling forge so they can visit you but your horse still has the benefit of being hot shod.

Cold shoeing Under this system the farrier carries with him a large variety of ready-made shoes. The set which best fits your horse is chosen and slight alterations made to obtain the closest fit possible.

How do you know whether your horse needs new shoes?

1. If the shoe has become loose or has been lost (cast) altogether.
2. If the shoe has worn thin and/or smooth.
3. If any of the foot has overgrown the shoe.
4. If the clenches have risen.

What happens when a horse is shod?

First of all the farrier will just look at the old shoes whilst on the horse. From this he can tell how the horse moves and whether any remedial shoeing is needed. He then removes the old shoes. The clenches are raised using a buffer and the shoe is eased off with the aid of pincers.

The next stage is to trim the wall and remove any ragged pieces of the sole and frog using the drawing knife. If there is excessive overgrowth of the wall then the hoofcutters are used. the farrier then uses a rasp to ensure that the bearing surface of the hoof is level.

A shoe is then tried against the horse's foot, heated in the forge and held against the hoof using a pritchel. After a few seconds the shoe is removed and the farrier can see the brown mark left by the impression of the shoe. This shows where the foot and shoe are in contact, and the farrier can then see where any slight alterations need to be made.

Once he is satisfied with the fit, the relevant spaces for the toe and quarter clips are cut out using the drawing knife.

The shoe is then nailed on. The stronger the wall of a horse's foot, then the fewer nails are required to hold the shoe in place. However, the figure usually quoted is seven nails, four on the outside and three on the inside. It is vital that the nails are placed correctly, penetrating the foot between the white line and the outer edge. If they are incorrectly positioned they can cause pressure and lameness. One of the first nails to be driven in will be near the toe. The ends of the nails which penetrate the wall are twisted off; the small pieces which are left are known as the clenches. These are bedded down into the hoof wall — a small nick will have been made with the rasp under the nail so that the clench can be turned down. These are then tapped down and smoothed with the rasp.

To finish off, the clips are tapped back and then the rasp is run lighty around the wall to help prevent any cracking.

Fore shoes have toe clips and hind shoes have quarter clips.

Good farriers always make the shoes fit the horse, never the other way around. You do see some horses whose toes have been 'dumped' where the toe has been cut back so that it fits the shoe.

Once the farrier has finished take a look at the horse as he is standing still. You should not be able to see daylight between the shoe and the hoof — always look particularly closely at the heel region. The foot should have been reduced evenly all round and the heels of the shoes should not be too long nor too short. All the clenches should be in line, the places for the clips neatly cut and bedded down.

Types of shoe

The hunter shoe is one of the most common types and it is intended for horses moving quickly on grass, making sudden turns and changes of speed. It is therefore made of concave iron with a groove or fullering on the ground surface for a secure grip. The heels of the fore shoes are smoothed off (known as pencilling) to reduce the chances of the shoes being torn off if a hind foot catches a fore foot. To cut down the chances of an over-reach injury, the toes of the hind shoes are rolled (ie set back and bevelled off).

A front shoe — note the toe clip and the groove to give better grip.

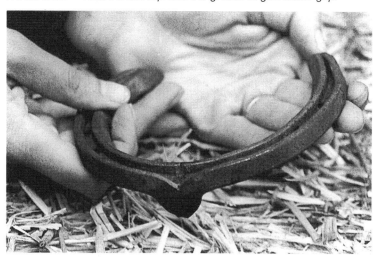

A hind shoe — note appearance of the toe which has been rolled to reduce the risk of an overreach injury.

Grass tips are half-length shoes used on animals turned out to grass. Their purpose is to help prevent the wall at the toe splitting. They also allow the frog to come into full action, essential for the foot's health, as the frog helps in circulation of the blood as well as being a shock absorber and anti-slip device.

Note the stud hole in the outside edge of the hind shoe.

Feather-edged shoes are fitted on horses liable to brushing. The inner edges of the shoes are thinner and fit close in under the wall.

Bathing a horse

In summer, horses often become sweaty after work, such as after a jumping lesson, and a bath is much appreciated. If you are showing your horse it is also a good idea to give him a bath the day before the event. It removes deeply embedded dirt and grease so allowing your horse's skin to breathe more easily. However, you should not bath your horse unless you can be sure of drying him properly, because horses are very susceptible to chills.

You will need plentiful supplies of warm water, sponges, towels, a sweat scraper and a horse shampoo. Using plenty of water applied with a sponge, wet the coat all over. Some horses who are used to being washed will stand quite happily while buckets of water are poured over them, or while a hosepipe is used. The method you use will depend on your horse.

Do not damp the horse's head yet — leave that until last. Apply the shampoo to the rest of the horse's body, using a sponge to rub in the shampoo and create a lather. Rinse off the shampoo very thoroughly — you may have to rinse more than once. Remove excess water with the sweat scraper and then use sponges and/or towels to remove any remaining water.

The horse's mane can be washed at the same time as his body. It is easiest to immerse the tail in a bucket of water, swish it around to clean it, rinse using clean water and then squeeze out the water by running your hand down the length of the tail. The bottom part of the tail can also be swirled around to remove excess water.

Use a clean sponge to wash the horse's head and do not use any shampoo. Be very careful and use your hand to shield the horse's eyes. Do not use the sweat scraper on the head or any other bony parts of the horse's body.

A towelling or summer sheet can be used to rub the horse's body dry whilst old towels can be used to dry off the legs. Pay particular attention to the heels. The horse should then be walked in the sunshine to dry if possible. Once the horse is dry brush him over with a clean body brush.

Clipping

This is the removal of part or all of the horse's winter coat. If a horse with a thick winter coat is worked he will sweat excessively, which means it is more difficult to dry the animal and so he is susceptible to chills. In addition, a heavily sweating horse will be distressed and

When clipping sensitive areas like the head, a small, quiet-running pair of clippers can be used.

it is more difficult to keep condition on him.

By clipping your horse you will be able to work him for longer periods and at a faster pace without undue distress (providing, of course, the horse is fit for the work you are asking him to do). It is much easier to keep a clipped horse clean and it is easier to dry him off, for example after hunting. However, if you remove some of the horse's natural winter coat you must substitute rugs and blankets to keep the horse warm.

Autumn will be heralded by the appearance of advertisements at saddlers and in your local paper offering clipping services. Depending on the individual horse, you may need to clip your horse two, three or four times during winter, so you will have to decide whether to pay someone else to clip the animal for you or invest in a pair of clippers and learn how to do it yourself! Ring round a few people who offer clipping. You will probably find that a full clip (when all the horse's coat is removed) will cost around £15-20. A set of clippers will set you back at least £150, but you will have several years' service from them.

Whoever is clipping your horse, it should not be done until his winter coat has grown (around October) and do not continue to clip once the summer coat has started to grow, usually no later than the last week of January.

Types of clip

Full All the coat is removed, eg, for horses hunting hard all winter. Usually a full clip is done for the first clip and then the hunter clip is

Horses and ponies who are working hard throughout the winter months may be hunter clipped — the saddle patch and legs are left unclipped but the winter coat is removed from everywhere else.

used for subsequent clips.

Hunter clip The saddle patch is left on to prevent the back becoming sore and the legs are left unclipped up to the elbows (forelegs) and thighs (hind legs). Leaving hair on the legs protects them against cold, thorns and mud.

Blanket So called as a blanket-shaped patch of hair is left over the body. Hair is removed from the neck and belly. This clip is useful for horses who are being lightly worked.

Trace clip Hair is removed from the belly and sides to trace height, top of the legs and under the neck. Horses or ponies who have to live out but are also working can have trace clips. Sometimes a low trace clip is given so that less hair is removed from the horse's sides.

You should not clip inside your horse's ears, because the hair there acts as a filter for dirt and protects against the cold. Do not remove a horse's whiskers either, as these are his chief organ of touch.

Trim a horse's feathers with scissors and comb not clippers. In winter particularly it is advisable to let your horse retain his natural feather; after all it is nature's way of letting water drain off his legs without collecting in the heels where it could cause cracked heels.

Above *A blanket clip leaving a blanket of hair on the pony's back.*

Below *A low trace clip.*

Above *A trace clip — here more hair has been removed as the pony's work involves longer and faster sessions.*

Below *Variation on a theme — here the hair has been removed from the pony's belly, neck and along part of his flanks. His hindquarters still have the winter coat.*

Before you clip

It is easier to clip a clean horse than one with a greasy coat, so the first requirement is a clean, dry animal. Bandage the tail. Make sure you have an assistant on hand to hold the horse. Horse hair gets everywhere when you are clipping, so dress in old clothes, or wear an overall and head covering.

Try to clip in daylight hours and use a stable which is well lit. Collect your kit together: clippers, spare blades, oil, brush to clean clippers, body brush to remove cut hair from horse at regular intervals, blanket to put over your horse for warmth once you start removing his coat, saddle soap to mark out saddle patch and legs. For grey horses use blue tailor's chalk to mark clipping lines.

Let your horse become accustomed to the sound of the clippers before you start using them. If you do not know how your horse reacts to clipping you will have to run the clippers near him to gauge his reaction. For horses who are wary of the noise it is worth spending a week or so letting the horse get used to them before starting to clip.

Despite such preparatory measures some horses do become very upset and consequently are difficult to clip. If you really do need to clip an awkward horse, then it is possible for the horse to be tranquillized by the vet.

How to clip

Check that the clippers are clean and working. Keep them well oiled throughout the whole process, and stop at intervals to clean them. If they start to get hot then stop, because hot blades will upset your horse. Once the clippers have cooled down you can continue the process. Stop clipping if your horse starts to sweat.

The weight of the clipping head should provide all the necessary pressure, so there is no need to push or force them along the coat. Always work against the hair growth, using long sweeping strokes, and keeping the clippers flat against the hair.

The tension of the blades should be just enough so that they clip. Do not try to clip with dull blades and have a pair of sharpened blades as spares. Be careful that neither you nor your horse can trip over any wires and that the horse cannot step on any wiring.

Before you switch on the clippers run them up the horse's neck, then switch on and run them for 30 seconds or so. The easiest place to start is the horse's neck but exactly where will depend on which clip you are doing. Run the clippers up the neck and let the next line overlap the first. Continue to remove the coat on the neck as appropriate.

If you are trace clipping, move from the neck to the trace lines, which can be marked with soap or chalk if you are uncertain about clipping in a straight line. Start just in front of the stifle and aim to finish at the front of the shoulder. You can then clip the horse's belly, but take care as some horses are particularly ticklish in this area.

When clipping around the horse's elbows ask a friend to pull your horse's leg forwards to make it easier. Always clip against the hair, stretching the skin when necessary to keep it smooth.

As you work along the horse's chest, take care to clip against the hair growth. You'll find that your sweeps with the clippers will be shorter here as the lay of the coat changes direction.

If you are trace clipping, you can check that both sides are level by using a piece of string from withers/neck/loin etc to trace line to measure the depth.

Mark the hind legs at the same angles as the forelegs and clip from back to front. Move the tail to one side so that you can tidy up the back and inside of the hindlegs. If you are giving your horse a full clip it's common practice to leave a triangle of hair at the top of the tail.

Always be careful when clipping out the neck that you do not go too close to the mane. Some horses are fine about being clipped except when it comes to having their heads attended to, so you may need to change to a smaller and quieter pair of clippers. It is important to keep the horse's head still. Start clipping on the cheekbone moving towards the eye. Be very careful when clipping in this area and cover the eye when you are clipping near it. Work from nose to ears, taking great care when clipping the horse's ears.

> The secret of good horsemanship is attention to detail. Don't just look at your horse — *look* and *see*!

Stand back and look at the horse from all angles to make sure any lines are level. This also lets you see where a little tidying up is needed — and remember that a clip always looks better after a couple of days!

If you do decide to clip your own horse it is wise to have a more experienced person standing by to sort out any problems and lend a hand if necessary. Clipping is something to be learnt by practice rather than reading about it.

Signs of health and disease

Owning a horse is a major responsibility accompanied by pleasures, chores and its times of trouble and distress. If your horse becomes ill then it is a worrying period, as well as often being costly in terms of veterinary fees. However, you have chosen to have a living creature relying upon you and so you must learn to recognize his way of telling you that all is not well.

Before you can tell whether a horse is ill you need to know about his appearance and behaviour under normal circumstances. This is where it pays to spend time just being with your horse, watching him and getting to know his funny little quirks and habits.

> When attaching leadropes with spring clips to headcollars have the moving part of the clip away from the jawbone. Otherwise a nasty injury can be caused if the clip sticks into the horse.

For instance, you have had your horse for a month, he is out at grass and he has always shown an interest in your arrival in the morning at feeding time. One morning you arrive at the field and he is standing in a corner of the field, looking dejected and not at all inclined to come to your call. Your immediate thought may be, 'Oh, no, I'm already running late and now the horse is playing up!' However, what you should be thinking — and what hopefully you will train yourself to think — is, 'That's funny — what's wrong?'

So what are the signs of a healthy and an unhealthy horse?

1 Horses are generally alert, taking an interest in their surroundings. If they can't be bothered with you and look dejected or miserable, something is wrong.

2 Healthy coats have a bloom on them whereas the coats of sick animals are dull and 'staring'. Obviously a horse who is kept at grass will not have the same sheen on his coat as one who lives in, is thoroughly groomed every day and is in show condition. The coat should not be excessively scurfy.

3 A horse's skin should be supple and loose. If you pinch the skin and it stays 'pinched' that's a sign of dehydration. Skin which is tight can also indicate general malnutrition.

4 Look at the horse's eyes; they should be bright. If you turn back the lids the membranes will be revealed. Pale salmon pink membranes are a healthy sign, other colours denote trouble; eg, deep red membranes would indicate fever.

5 If a horse is sweating unnecessarily, particularly if he constantly looks around at his flank and tries to kick out at his stomach, then alarm bells should ring. (In this example colic is likely to be the problem and veterinary help is required.)

6 Any variation from the normal temperature of a horse should be acted upon. Call the vet! The usual temperature is 100–101°F (38°C) and this is taken in the rectum using a veterinary thermometer (these can be obtained from your vet). Grease the thermometer with petroleum jelly, lift the tail and gently insert the thermometer into the horse's rectum, using a rotating action. Do not let go of the thermometer!

When you buy the thermometer, ask how long you should leave it in position when taking a horse's temperature. Once the thermometer has been withdrawn and read, sterilize it before returning it to your first aid kit.

7 Check the horse's breathing, either by standing to the side and counting the flank movements or by holding your hand close to the nostrils so you can feel each breath. At rest the normal respiration rate is 8-15 per minute with the breathing being even and regular. The nostrils and ribs should only move slightly, the horse's breathing should not be laboured.

Obviously exercise will increase the respiration rate — if you are an aerobics participant you will know how important your respiration and pulse rates are. It is the recovery rate which indicates the fitness of both animals and humans.

8 The horse's pulse can be felt on the inner surface of his jaw, where the facial artery passes under the jaw or at the median artery which is found on the inside of the foreleg, level with the horse's elbow. At rest a normal pulse would be 35-40 beats per minute. Stress and excitement will increase the pulse.

If you take up long-distance riding you would be wise to invest in a stethoscope (I bought mine through the veterinary surgery) as the horse's pulse rate and recovery rate is important during training and the actual long-distance riding events.

9 The horse's body should be well covered with flesh. Animals in poor condition often have ribs and haunches showing, their quarters are not rounded and their necks are scrawny. There should not be any heat or swelling in the limbs. As part of your daily grooming process and the overall daily check you should give your horse, look for any swellings or abnormalities. Is that offside knee slightly swollen? Compare it with the other knee to help you decide.

10 A healthy animal will pass droppings regularly, eight or nine times a day. The colour of the droppings varies according to the horse's diet, greenish if he's out at grass, golden if he lives in and receives short feed. The boluses of the droppings should break on contact with the ground.

If an animal only passes a few droppings there can be serious problems, such as an impacted bowel, which requires urgent veterinary attention. The droppings of a horse who lives out may be looser than those of a stabled horse.

11 Urine should also be passed several times a day by a healthy horse, and should either be virtually colourless or a pale yellow. Signs of blood in the urine or difficulty in staling should be investigated further.

12 Another big clue to how your horse is feeling is his consumption of food and water. A horse should drink in between six and ten gallons of water daily — one of the disadvantages of an automatic watering machine in a stable is that it is difficult to monitor how much a horse is drinking.

13 Uneaten food or untouched haynets are other warning signs. If your horse is a fussy eater it is even more important for you to know his habits in order to distinguish between a normal day and one when he genuinely is not feeling well.

If the horse has difficulty in eating, have his teeth checked because they can become sharp and may need rasping. A yearly check by your vet should be part of your horse's routine care.

First aid kit

The time is bound to come when you need to administer first aid to your horse — perhaps to deal with a small wound — so it is sensible to keep a well-stocked kit handy at your horse's home and to carry the kit with you when you are out and about at shows.

Keep the items clean by storing them in a clearly marked container with a snap shut lid; a large ice-cream carton or biscuit tin is fine. Have the telephone number of your vet written on the container and keep some change for the telephone with the kit, so you do not waste time in the case of an emergency. Your kit should contain:

Wound powder A dry powder such as sulphonamide, plus waterproof dressings such as green oils which may be needed in preference to dry powders if the horse lives out.

Antiseptic ointment Eg Protocon for use as a dressing, plus an antiseptic such as Dettol for sterilizing bowls and thermometers after use.

The contents of a typical stable first aid kit, complete with a snap-shut lidded container marked with the telephone numbers of your vet and doctor.

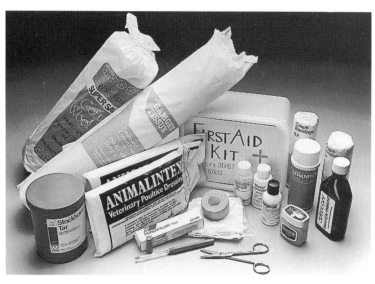

Bandages A supply of plain, crepe and elasticated bandages, eg, two of each should cover your needs. Once the bandages have been removed from their packing keep them clean by storing them in polythene bags. Stable bandages are also useful as an over-bandage to keep everything clean and in position.

Cotton wool Used for swabbing wounds. Make sure an opened pack stays clean.

Surgical gauze Powder or ointment can be put on to gauze and this is then placed over the wound with a cotton wool pad and a bandage applied to keep the dressing in place. Do not apply cotton wool pads directly on to wounds as pieces of cotton wool will stick to the flesh.

Scissors A blunt-ended pair.

Bowls Stainless steel ones for holding fluids, instruments etc. These are easy to sterilize after use.

Poultices Ready-made ones are available, some of which are suitable for use as hot or cold poultices and which can be re-used.

Sponge One of the easiest ways to clean a wound is to run water over it. The best way to do this is by using a hosepipe but as one is not always available use a sponge. However, it is important that the sponge is clean. Some sponges can be boiled.

Salt Used to make up a saline solution for cleaning wounds.

Ready-made poultices are easy to use — and some are re-usable.

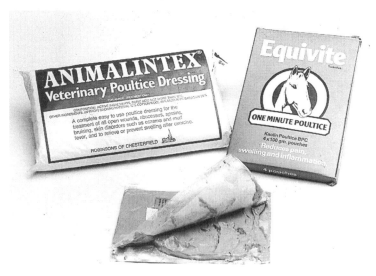

Wounds

There are various types of wounds:

Bruised The skin is not actually broken, although the vessels underneath are ruptured.

Clean cut Generally caused by a very sharp edge such as glass. Bleeding is severe.

Torn For example, if a horse becomes caught up in barbed wire the flesh tears as the horse frees himself. Often stitching is needed.

Puncture These wounds cannot be seen although they cause serious problems. For instance, the horse may tread on a nail and although the entrance hole to the wound is small the nail penetrates deep into the tissues, leaving dirt and germs often resulting in an abscess.

Attach pieces of breakable string to your tying-up rings and tie the leadrope through these rather than on to a fixed object. Then if the horse panics while he is tied up he can pull back and be free. If he pulled back against a solid object he would panic more and injure himself.

Your immediate priorities are to stop the bleeding and to prevent infection. With anything other than a small wound you should seek veterinary attention — the killer disease tetanus can be contracted via the smallest of cuts and your horse needs to be protected against

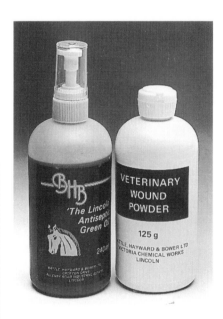

Green oils and powder — two types of dressings for wounds.

this. He should already have an annual anti-tetanus jab, but boosters are always a sensible precaution.

Clean the wound thoroughly — you may have to clip away the hair around the wound to make this easier. Do not start prodding about in the wound, especially if the wound is near a joint, as you could rupture the sac containing joint oil. If the cut is deep or you suspect a puncture wound, call the vet. The latter needs to be opened so any debris can be drained out by use of a poultice, but this calls for professional attention.

For small wounds, once you are sure they are clean and dry, apply a dressing as suitable, ie, waterproof if the animal lives out. If you need to apply a dressing and bandage, remember that there may be some swelling, so do not apply the bandage too tightly.

Saddle sores and girth galls

The former are caused by badly fitting saddles which result in friction and/or pressure, whilst girth galls are the result of girths being done up too tightly and wrinkling the skin. Bits of mud on the girth or a girth which is hard through dried sweat can also rub and cause soreness.

Both these injuries result in soreness and the only way to ease this is to stop working the horse until the gall or sore has healed. You must prevent a recurrence by removing the cause of the injury. Saline solution or witch-hazel applied to the girth area helps harden the skin, a precautionary measure if your horse is in soft condition and you are bringing him back into work.

FEEDING

At one time horsey people used to talk about the 'art of feeding'. Now feeding is an art *and* a science. Phrases like 'digestible energy' and 'calcium to phosphorus ratio' sit alongside old favourites such as 'feed plenty of bulk' and 'water before feeding'.

Bags of feed now list the ingredients and their feed values, there is a host of information sheets available from feed manufacturers and equine nutritionists offer consultancy services. Although there is a great deal of information around from which you and your horse can benefit, there is still an important place for common sense and observing your horse. Every horse is an individual with its own pecular feeding habits, likes and dislikes. Equip yourself with all the information on feeding that you can, but always remember to deal with each horse's needs separately.

Horses need food to put on flesh and repair body wastes, for development and as an energy supply for work. However, the food needs to be broken down by the animal's digestive system into a form which is useful to the horse.

The whole process of digestion starts with the lips and teeth. The lips gather food and the molars (the back teeth) grind the food. The incisors, at the front of the horse's mouth, are cutting teeth, used, for instance, as the horse grazes. As the molars grind the food saliva is produced, which aids the passage of the food along the gullet into the stomach. For its size the horse has a small stomach — with a capacity of 2-4 gallons. In their natural state horses eat little and often, preferring to keep their stomachs half-full for the majority of the time. One of the guidelines for feeding domesticated horses is to imitate nature.

Up to the point where the food reaches the stomach there will have been few changes to the food, but when it is mixed with gastric juices the process of digestion starts in earnest. The food is acidified and various enzymes start work; eg, pepsin which begins to break down the protein in the food, and lipase which affects the fats and oils in the food.

Proteins, lipids (ie, fats and oils) and carbohydrates form the bulk of the digestible food. However, the food which horses eat also contains water, vitamins and minerals.

From the stomach, the food passes to the small intestine which has three parts to it and is about 22 metres long! The first section is known as the duodenum. It is here that bile secreted from the liver helps the digestive process by emulsifying the lipids so they are more readily absorbed.

Secretions from the pancreas also flow into the duodenum, and these and the bile turn the acidic contents of the stomach alkaline. Other enzymes are also coming into play, breaking down proteins into amino acids and starch into glucose.

The next section is the jejunum, the major part of the small intestine. Here the food is mixed with more digestive juices and minerals, vitamins, amino acids and glucose are absorbed via the intestinal wall into the blood stream.

Food residues then pass through the final part of the small intestine — the ileum — to the caecum and then colon of the large intestine. Although this is not as long as the small intestine, its volume is considerably greater. It can take several days for the food to be broken down in the colon. Bacteria live in both the caecum and colon and these are needed as the microbes contain enzymes which the horse does not have. These enzymes help to break down the main constituents of grass and hay and also digest any fats, protein or carbohydrate which have not been absorbed.

Unfortunately there are 'design problems' with the horse's digestive tract. For instance there is a right-angled bend in the colon and large particles of food can become trapped here resulting in colic. Worm damage can also result in dead tissue and a restricted flow of food residues leading to blockages.

It takes three to four days for food to pass through a horse. The final stage is for the waste products of digestion to be formed into balls of dung which pass through the rectum and anus.

In order for your horse to have a balanced diet, his feed must contain the following essentials:

Carbohydrates and fats The main energy sources, ie, the fuels which allow your horse to grow and run.

Proteins These are vital for the maintenance, growth and repair of animal tissues.

Minerals Eg, salt, magnesium, iron, needed for a wide range of biochemical processes in the body.

Vitamins Important for normal growth and maintenance, present in fresh grown food such as grass.

Water Needed for the shape and form of every cell, for many digestive processes and metabolism, and for numerous other jobs, eg, lubricating joints and eyes.

In the league table of a balanced diet, water is the most important, followed by energy, vital for a horse to function. It is needed to maintain blood pressure and the action of the heart, for growth and to maintain body temperature as well as many other functions.

Carbohydrates Provide the major source of energy and these include sugars (molasses), starch (cereals), cellulose and hemi-cellulose (hay and forages). Not all the energy in the food is of use to the horse; that which is useful is known as the digestible energy. In order to know which foods are most valuable to your horse look at the breakdowns given on feed bags. Most people think oats are the best energizing food, yet molassed sugar beet has a higher digestible energy value.

Protein If a horse's diet does not contain enough energy, ie, there are insufficient carbohydrates and fats, then the horse will use protein as an energy source. However, protein first has to be broken down and this process involves the animal using energy. A horse suffering from an energy deficiency is lethargic, dull and lifeless and loses condition and weight.

Each particular organ and tissue in your horse's body will have its own proteins. Most bodily functions are affected by proteins and they also provide resistance to disease. As protein is not a fuel source for the horse there is no need to increase protein intake if the horse's workload increases.

Proteins are made from amino acids and of the 25 acids in nature the horse needs 22. Amino acids are split into non-essential, which can be synthesized by the horse itself as his body demands, and essential, which must be provided in the diet if the horse is to remain healthy.

Minerals There are 16 which are considered essential. Virtually all feeds contain minerals but the amounts vary. Some feeds such as horse and pony cubes have been specially formulated to contain a consistent amount of minerals. In addition there are mineral and vitamin supplements available, but never feed more than one supplement at a time and do not exceed the recommended levels.

Minerals which the horse needs include calcium, found in ground limestone, molassed sugar beet; phosphorus, found in cereals, bran, bone meal; salt, which may be added to the feed or given in the form of salt licks; magnesium, eg, in linseed cake; potassium, where that available in forage is usually sufficient; sulphur, which usually occurs in proteins.

You may hear talk of trace minerals, eg, iron, cobalt, manganese, selenium, which are needed in the diet. Most feeds already have trace minerals present.

Vitamins Also required in minute quantities. Many are widely found in existing horse feeds.

Types of feed

Hay

This may be meadow hay, cut from permanent pasture and usually containing a wide variety of grasses, or seed hay, a specially sown crop. Seed hay is more expensive — good quality meadow hay should be sufficient for your horse.

Hay can be bought from local farmers or corn and hay merchants; you should be able to find the addresses in the Yellow Pages or through advertisements in your local paper. Usually the cheapest way to buy hay is to wait until harvest and buy it off the field from a local farmer. However, you must have space to store this hay until it is ready to be eaten. Once hay has been cut and baled it has to go through some chemical processes before it is ready to be eaten — this is why you should not feed new hay. It takes a minimum of two months and usually more before the hay is ready. Ideally hay which is less than six months old should not be fed.

One of the first questions you should ask the farmer or hay merchant is the age of the hay. Then smell the hay, dividing a bale so you can smell the inside too. It should be sweet and clean, not mouldy.

The colour of the hay will vary according to the mixture of grasses but should be greenish to a light browny-green. As hay becomes older so it becomes more brown. Avoid hay which is yellow (indicating weathering), brown (showing that the grass has been cut too late and incorrectly stored) or dark brown (mow-burnt hay which has over-heated whilst in the stack).

Avoid dusty hay. A few thistles in a bale are acceptable but if there are lots of weeds do not buy the hay as it will have been cut from poor land. Feel the hay — it should be crisp but not spiky.

Let your horse give his opinion of the hay too. There is no point in committing yourself to 60 bales for winter if he refuses to eat it.

Haylage

Some horses and ponies are allergic to the dust and fungal spores which develop during the making and storing of hay. For this reason, various alternatives to hay which are dust-free have been developed.

Grass is cut when at its best, allowed to half-dry and then pressed and sealed in plastic bags. The drying process then continues in a dust-free environment and the end result is a very palatable product, which also has a high nutritional value. It is therefore not necessary to give hard feed (depending on work-load). However, as haylage costs more than ordinary hay, your feed bills are not necessarily reduced.

Small-holed haynets are used when feeding haylage as it is easily digested and takes little time to consume. Consequently horses fed haylage will not spend as much time pulling at their haynets as with traditional hay and may become bored more easily without food to

occupy them.
Careful storage of haylage packs is needed because if the bags are punctured then the exposed part becomes mouldy. This can be thrown away and the rest of the undamaged haylage used.

Chaff

Hay or oat straw may be chopped up to make chaff. This is usually added to a feed to slow down a horse who bolts his feed.

Bran

A by-product of the milling process of wheat, bran should be broad-flaked, dry and floury. It is one of the traditional horse feeds, although modern opinion is that it has little feed value.

Oats

They should be plump, heavy and sweet smelling, free from dirt or dust. Oats should be bruised, rolled or crushed so that the hard shell of the seed is broken, exposing the kernel to the digestive juices. Do not store crushed oats for longer than three weeks as they begin to lose their feed value.

Cubes

There are a variety of cubes or nuts on the market now, for all kinds of purposes, eg, stud cubes, event cubes, horse and pony nuts. These

Bran should be broad-flaked, dry and floury.

compounded horse feeds have been specially formulated to provide a balanced diet for the particular type of
animal they are aimed at — so there is no point or value in
feeding racehorse cubes to your horse.

Cereals, molasses, vitamins and minerals are contained in the cubes
but they can become rather boring. Apples, carrots and chaff mixed
with them will add interest and ensure adequate mastication and
salivation, without upsetting the balance of the cubes.

Coarse mixes

These ready-mixed and nutritionally balanced foods are useful for
new owners. Mixes vary according to their use, eg, riding horse mix,
pony mix. They contain the normal feedstuffs but you are relieved of
the duty of getting the balance correct. In addition, coarse mixes save
on storage space.

Extruded feeds

In recent years a revolutionary new feed processing method, known
as dry extrusion, has resulted in the production of extruded feeds.
Basically, the feed ingredients are pressure-cooked so they expand
rapidly and emerge rather like popcorn. As the process is so quick
the ingredients retain their maximum goodness and the availability
of the nutrients is enhanced. This means that the feeds have a much
higher digestible factor than 'normal' feeds.

*Coarse mixes are a good choice for first-time owners as they provide a ready-
mixed and balanced diet.*

Sugar beet pulp before soaking. Never feed this dry to your horse — always soak it, whether it's in shreds or cube form.

This method of processing was developed in the USA by a group of leading equine nutritionists and horse people. At the same time they initiated a unique concept of feeding which regards the horse's diet as a nutritional pyramid, built up according to the horse's daily requirements.

For more information on this, and advice on providing a balanced diet for your horse, you can contact Triple Crown Horse Feeds, Portfield, Chichester, West Sussex PO19 2NT.

Other manufacturers are now making extruded feeds so ask your feed merchant for more advice.

Sugar beet

Available in shreds or cubes, sugar beet must be thoroughly soaked before being fed to the horse. Otherwise it may cause choking or it may swell in the stomach. It should be soaked overnight in at least twice its own volume of water. Once the beet has been soaked it should be used within a day or it will start to ferment. Molassed sugar beet is a useful energy source as it has a higher digestible energy value than oats. It is also used for putting flesh on thin horses.

Barley

Boiled barley is often fed in winter to keep flesh on horses. However,

You need to know precisely how much feed your horse is receiving so that you can adjust his feed according to circumstances, eg reduce intake if the horse is off work.

it has to be boiled for several hours so it may not be economical or worth the effort if you only have one horse.

Maize
A fattening and heating food, this should only be fed in small amounts.

Linseed oil meal
Linseed is nutritious, rich in proteins and oils. However the linseed has to be soaked overnight and then boiled to produce either a linseed jelly or tea which is added to the feed. To save time and effort you could feed linseed oil meal which has all the properties of cooked linseed.

Feeding considerations

1 Try to imitate the horse's natural way of feeding, ie, little and often. Feeds which are too large can cause digestive problems such as colic.
2 Feed plenty of bulk, eg, hay. Always give hay before hard feed as this will get the horse's digestive juices going and his stomach working.
3 Water before you feed. Ideally your horse should have fresh, clean water available at all times so he can drink whenever he wishes. If you come back from a ride offer your horse water before giving him any

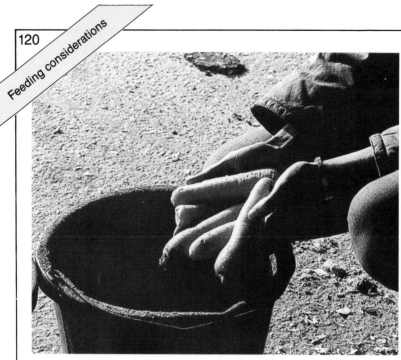

Above *Succulents such as carrots are a welcome addition to the horse's diet.*

Below *Store your feed in vermin-proof bins if possible.*

feed. If the horse has a long drink after a feed then the undigested food will be washed out of his stomach and this could lead to digestive problems.

4 Feed according to age, weight, temperament, breed, work. Young growing horses and pregnant mares have different require- ments from older horses, whilst those in hard work need more than resting animals or those in light work.

5 Feed at the same time every day, because horses are creatures of routine and soon learn their feeding pattners: they have very accurate, in-built clocks! If a feed does not appear at the usual and expected time it can cause distress to your horse. In addition, irregular feeding will not be advantageous to your horse's digestive system.

6 Feed something succulent, eg, carrots and apples, each day to add variety and interest to the feed.

7 Following on from the fact that your horse's digestion copes better with small, regular feeds, make any changes to the horse's diet very gradually, over a period of days.

8 Use only good quality feed and hay.

9 Measure out your horse's feed accurately, and keep a record of his daily feed so that if someone has to feed him in your absence they will know exactly what has to be given.

10 Keep all feeding utensils clean.

11 Store your feed in metal or plastic, vermin-free bins with the contents of each bin clearly labelled.

12 Soak sugar beet for at least 12 hours before use.

13 Do not leave uneaten food in the manger, and remember that if a horse is off his feed it is a sign that something is wrong with his health.

14 As a rough guide, a horse needs 2.5 per cent of his body weight in food every day split into 60 per cent roughage, eg, hay, and 40 per cent concentrates, eg, oats. As a horse works harder so the proportion of concentrates in his diet increases and the roughage decreases accordingly. Measuring tapes can now be bought which are graded so that you can read off the horse's measurements around the girth and his consequent weight and food requirements.

Alternatively there is a fairly accurate way of calculating your horse's weight: measure his girth in inches, then measure the distance from the point of the prominent hip bone of the pelvis to the shoulder in inches. Then insert these values into the following equation:

$$\text{Weight in kilogrammes} = \frac{(\text{chest girth})^2 \times \text{length, hip to shoulder}}{660}$$

THE HORSE WORLD

Having your own horse opens up a whole new world of competition and fun. Now, instead of being an envious onlooker at the local show, you can enjoy taking part.

To make the most of these new opportunities you need to prepare yourself and your horse properly. A show is the place where all your homework is put to the test, not the place to teach your horse to jump properly! So often people disappoint themselves at shows because they go with high, and often unjustified, expectations. It is just not feasible to expect to win the first novice jumping class you enter when you have only had the horse a couple of days. Successful competitive partnerships are built up over time. Any rider who consistently does well at shows has put in considerable time and effort beforehand. As soon as you start looking at show schedules, you will realize that there is a tremendous choice of riding activities. Let us look at the disciplines and classes available.

Affiliated competitions

Various events such as dressage, show-jumping competitions and horse trials are run according to the rules of their governing bodies. These are therefore official or affiliated competitions, eg, affiliated to the British Show Jumping Association or official British Horse Society Horse Trials. To enter these competitions you need to be a member of the relevant society and your horse has to be registered. This naturally involves a fee.

As a new owner and presumably a relatively novice rider you are not likely to be ready for such competitions yet, but this information is provided here so you can appreciate the difference between affiliated and unaffiliated classes.

Unaffiliated competitions

Most local shows and small gymkhanas are organized by local riding clubs, village committees and so on, and their classes are not held

in conjunction with the major equestrian bodies. Some
classes, such as showing competitions, are connected with
the major showing societies, but this is generally made clear
in the schedule.

However, with unaffiliated classes there are still some distinctions
amongst the classes in order to ensure some fairness of competition.
For example, classes are often divided according to the age of rider,
height of pony or horse, experience of the horse, ie, 'Novice jumping
class, riders 16 years and under, ponies 14.2 hh and under, not to have
won more than £10 in any jumping competition'.

As you can see, there are immediate problems here for adult riders
of ponies because the class is divided according to the rider's age.
Luckily many show organizers are now realizing that lots of adults are
relatively new competitors and so are providing veterans classes or
are simply not including the age limitation.

With unaffiliated shows where previous winnings are brought into
the equation (as in the example above), the organizers are relying
on people's honesty. However, you will always find some people whose
horses are well out of novice classes yet they still enter!

Not all horsey sports are competitive in the strictest terms. For
instance long distance riding does not usually put you into direct
competition with other riders. Instead you are in competition with time
and distance.

Whatever your interest and age, and whatever type of horse you
own, there is something for you in the world of horses.

Hacking

This is a major activity in the horse world, and of course non-
competitive. Riding purely for pleasure may be the major reason you
have your own horse. Hacking can be made even more enjoyable by
joining together with other horse owners and exploring bridleways or
going on picnic or pub rides.

If you live near a beach check with the local authority about its use
by horse riders. Similarly, in areas where there is Forestry Commission
land it may be necessary to buy a permit to give you access to the
forest rides.

Make use of Ordnance Survey maps of your local area to pinpoint
bridleways. Some may not have been used recently and so are
overgrown or blocked. In some cases the owners of land through which
bridleways pass try to prevent the right of way being used. However,
with the ever-increasing traffic on our roads, riders need to do all they
can to keep bridleways open. Your local BHS Bridleways Officer or
the local authority will give help and advice if you find that local
landowners are trying to block or close bridleways. In many areas riders
have joined together to form bridleways groups in order to keep routes

Take care when riding along country lanes, and make sure you know the Highway Code.

open and to campaign for new provisions. Such groups are also a good way of making new horsey friends.

In company with other riders you may like to ride further afield, eg, day rides, planning your routes to take in both on and off road riding. Such excursions can also be extended to take in overnight stops. Careful planning with advance visits is needed to ensure all parts of the proposed route are open and overnight accommodation for your horse is suitable.

You will need to ensure that you and your horse are fit enough for these kind of trips — don't be over-ambitious. Fifteen to 20 miles per day would be a sensible distance to begin with, depending, of course, on the type of terrain in your area.

There are holidays available now which enable you and your horse to explore parts of Britain. Usually the routes are planned by the organizers, maps are provided, your overnight stops are booked and your luggage is taken on as part of the package. Arrangements can vary, so check with the individual companies. Details of such holidays can be found in the advertising sections of the national equine press.

If you prefer to be more independent, it is possible to obtain information from the British Horse Society on bed and breakfast stops for horses and riders throughout Britain.

Many riding holiday centres also allow riders with their own horses. Again, depending on the centre you can 'do your own thing', join in

Trekking numnahs like this are great for carrying supplies for picnic rides.

the organized rides and lessons for the week, or have occasional instruction and just use the centre as a base for exploring the surrounding countryside.

One of the investments you may like to make if you undertake longer rides is a trekking numnah or a saddle-bag. The latter is usually smaller and so would be more suitable for carrying gear on shorter rides. Saddle-bags can be attached to your saddle via the D-rings close to the cantle.

Trekking numnahs are much larger than normal numnahs and resemble saddle cloths rather than numnahs. They have two large pockets which are positioned behind the saddle flap on either side. Line the pockets with plastic bags to prevent the contents becoming wet, and pack them so that the weight is distributed evenly.

For day rides you can carry your horse's headcollar easily — take the noseband off the bridle and let the horse wear his headcollar under his bridle. The lead rope can be put up as shown overleaf and attached to a D-ring on the saddle.

Keep your map in a polythene bag or a proper map carrier as used by walkers, to protect against rain and keep the map in better condition. Regular use of your local OS map can soon result in it becoming torn and dog-eared.

It is a sensible precaution to attach little metal discs with your name and telephone number on to your horse's saddle and bridle. Then if

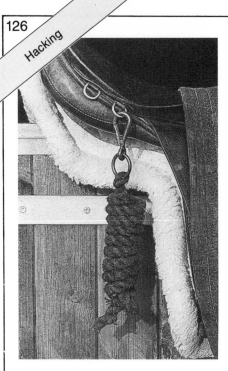

If you need to carry a lead rope it can be attached as shown or clipped to the ring close to the saddle pommel.

you part company and the horse is caught later by a stranger at least the person will have a contact point. Always carry some identification and a telephone number on your own person as well, just in case you do have a fall which knocks you out. Such information will provide anyone who finds you with the relevant details.

Another sensible precaution is to tell someone at your stables where you are going and how long you expect to be out. When riding out alone it is wise not to jump any obstacles you may find. If you do fall off and injure yourself you could be in serious trouble, so leave such activities for when you have a riding companion.

If you are planning a day ride remember to take with you a headcollar and rope; money, including small change for the telephone; personal identification including phone numbers; waterproofs/fly repellent depending on the weather; food and drink for yourself (try to plan your route to take in watering points for your horse); hoofpick; mini first aid kit for you and your horse (eg plasters, pain-killers, wound powder); map and container; watch.

You can share equipment with your riding companion. If you undertake longer excursions your equipment list will expand accordingly. Back-up plans will also need to be made to ensure bulky gear and your horse's feed are taken to overnight stopping places. You also need to provide for horse transport in case one of your horses goes lame or is ill during the trip.

Do not be over-ambitious with your mileage and allow plenty of time for the journey. If you do get lost or have to follow an unexpected and lengthy diversion then hopefully you will not have run out of daylight! On longer trips or day rides when the daylight hours are not so long, make sure you carry a torch and fluorescent bands for you and your horse (these can be attached to the horse's legs and tail).

Long-distance riding

If you enjoy longer hacks and expeditions you may like to add the extra element of competition against time and distance which long-distance riding offers.

There are two organizations involved in LDR in Britain: the Long Distance Riding Group of the British Horse Society and the Endurance Horse and Pony Society of Great Britain (see appendix for addresses). Both groups organize various grades of long-distance rides at venues all over the country. The different types of ride are:

Pleasure rides

These are over shorter distances, eg, 15-20 miles, and are intended as an introduction to the sport. Membership of the organizing society is not needed in order to take part in pleasure rides. Indeed some pleasure rides are organized by local riding clubs or bridleways groups as fund-raising events and so are often re-named sponsored rides.

Riders in pleasure rides complete the set course at their own speed (as a guideline you would not normally expect to take more than three hours to finish a 15 mile course) and their horses are not subject to scrutiny by the ride vet.

Competitive rides

These take various forms, from 25 mile rides to endurance feats such as 100 miles in 24 hours! Rides are graded according to the average speed at which you travel, eg, the British Horse Society's Bronze Buckle qualifying ride calls for 20 miles at 6½ mph, whilst at the BB Final you need to complete 30 miles at 7 mph.

However, there is more to long-distance riding than just completing the distance within the time limit. Before you start, your horse will be checked by a vet. Notes are made of pulse and respiration rates, any lumps or bumps and the horse is trotted up to check soundness. If the vet has any doubt about the horse's ability to undertake the ride, you will not be allowed to start. Tack and shoes are also checked for suitability and fitting.

During the ride the vet may appear at checkpoints, and if necessary he will pull out any animal who appears distressed or lame. Once you finish your ride there is 30 minutes' grace before you have to present your horse to the vet again. If your horse's pulse and respiration rates are outside the accepted limits or he is lame, then you will be 'spun', ie, you will have failed to complete the ride. The great test in long-distance riding is producing a horse to the required fitness for whichever level you are competing at. Plus, of course, you build a tremendous partnership with your horse as your training necessitates a great deal of time being spent with him.

Dressage

People are often put off from entering dressage competitions as they think it is all too high-flying for them. Yet dressage tests are simply ways of examining how your horse's schooling is progressing, and as your partnership improves so you can stretch yourselves by entering the higher-level tests.

Dressage tests involve everyday riding manoeuvres such as transitions, riding circles, changing rein, so why not have a go? Start off with preliminary tests and you will find that as well as being enjoyable, the judge's comments will be helpful to your horsey education.

You will find that riding clubs often include dressage tests in their shows, and you can find out from the show schedule which test is required. Dressage test sheets cost just a few pence and are available

In trot, a two-time pace, there are two diagonals: this is the left diagonal, ie near-fore and off-hind. The right diagonal is off-fore and near-hind.

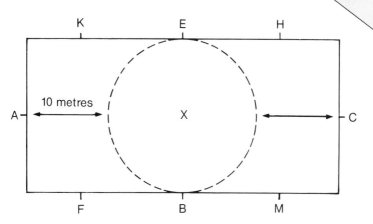

from the British Horse Society.

If you are worried about entering your first test then have a couple of lessons to work on your performance. You can accustom yourself and your horse to working in a dressage arena by marking out a correctly sized arena in your paddock — see the diagram above for the dimensions and lettering system. Do not ride the complete test too many times before the actual event, but just practise sections of it and only put it all together a couple of times before the day. If you practise the complete test too often, the horse starts to anticipate movements, which can work to your disadvantage on the actual competition day.

You will be allocated a time to ride your test by the show secretary a couple of days beforehand. Make sure you allow enough time to ride in and have your horse working well before you have to perform.

For the lower level tests you can have the test called out to you by a friend as you are riding. However, it is better if you can commit the test to memory. One way of doing this is to walk around your garden or field as if you are riding the test, saying, 'I'm now trotting, now I'm changing the rein showing a few lengthened strides', and so on. The neighbours may think you have gone crazy but it is a good way of memorizing your test!

Check that your tack is correct before you start working in. In straight dressage tests at preliminary level, only snaffle bits with either a cavesson, drop or flash noseband are allowed. Martingales should not be worn, neither should any protective boots or bandages be fitted. In a test which is part of a one-day event, grakle nosebands are permitted. If you are unsure about the allowed tack, check with the secretary before the event. The rules about carrying dressage whips and wearing spurs also cause confusion, so check first to avoid any upsets.

Most clubs arrange for a dressage collecting ring steward, who will be able to tell you whether the event is running to time or is ahead of schedule. Sometimes people do not arrive, so if you are ready you may be able to do your test earlier. However, do not be pressurized into riding earlier than your allocated time if you are not ready.

When it is your turn, ride up quietly to the judge's car and make sure your number can be seen or report to the judge's writer (assistant). Do not enter the actual dressage arena until the judge indicates he or she is ready for you — usually by pipping the car horn. Once you hear that you can enter and start the test. Do not make the mistake of hurrying, especially when you salute the judge. Take your time, smile and relax!

All you can do is ride to the best of your ability. You will be nervous, particularly if you have never ridden a test before, but try not to let panic overwhelm you because that is the surest way of forgetting the test.

If you do lose your way (you will no doubt hear the judge pip the car horn again if you go wrong), stay calm, go back to the point where you took the incorrect course and then carry on. Often the judge will say, 'You need to change the rein now/you should be cantering' and so on.

Remember to finish your test with a salute to the judge and then calmly walk out of the arena.

Show-jumping

One way to start off your show-jumping career is by taking part in the clear round (minimus) competitions which most shows include in their schedules. This gives you the chance to jump courses on a show ground without the added pressure of being in one of the major rings. Entries are taken on the day and everyone who achieves a clear round receives a rosette. Usually the courses are fairly small and if you have any problems you can always pay another entry fee and go round again. The only disadvantage with these classes is that sometimes the jumps are not as well-built as one would like, simply because the show's 'left-over' fences are used.

The next step would be novice classes. The height of the jumps is normally specified in the schedule, but usually they are not more than 2 ft 9 in (about 84 cm) in the first round. You will always have the opportunity to walk the course before you ride in the class, so make full use of this time to walk exactly the route you intend to ride.

The jumping order for the class will be determined by the order of the numbers on the board in the collecting ring. It is up to you to ask the collecting ring steward to put your number down and it is your responsibility to make sure you are ready to ride when it is your turn.

Allow yourself plenty of time to warm up on the flat and then to pop over the practice fence a few times. Your horse needs to be jumping freely and cleanly, going forwards well. When it is your turn, ride positively into the arena but do not make the mistake of starting before the bell is rung.

Keep calm and concentrate on the job in hand. If you knock down a fence, do not look back, but forget it and get on with the next one. If you bother about something which has already happened your chances of negotiating the next obstacles well are lessened.

Your round is not over until you have passed the finishing line — often the relief of reaching the last fence is so great that people forget to ride it properly and spoil an otherwise good round. However, your horse has gone, think back over the round and see what you can learn from, improve upon, or vow never to do again!

Hunter trials

These involve riding over fixed fences across country and are very exciting competitions. You may like to start off in the pairs classes if you have a friend with a reliable horse to partner you, or there are also novice classes.

The standard of the courses may vary. If the hunter trial is organized by the local hunt supporters club, the courses are generally well-built and flowing, the type you can really set sail at and enjoy. Other courses can be too twisty, trying to fit in too many jumps in only a small area. You would expect hunter trial courses to be a mile to a mile and a quarter (1.6-2km) in length. The fences do not have to be high to present problems as by clever use of the land's undulations a course-builder can put together a course which is inviting to the horse whilst being a little off-putting to the rider.

The course will take advantage of natural features like hedges, banks, water, drops and ditches, and will generally include a timed section which may involve opening and closing a gate.

Cross-country courses and hunter trial courses are pretty similar, although the competitions may differ in the standard of dress required. Some hunter trials insist on riders wearing hacking jackets whereas in cross-country competitions you can wear your colours, eg, rugby shirts.

The scoring for cross-country and hunter trials is different from that of show-jumping. In the latter if you have three refusals on the course you are eliminated. With cross-country you are eliminated if you have three refusals at the same fence. Many trials organizers are happy for you to continue your round even if you are eliminated, provided you make way for people coming behind you who are still in the competition.

One-day events

Local riding and pony clubs often organize these popular events for which entries flow thick and fast. The competition is made up of three elements — dressage, show-jumping and cross-country. Your penalties for each section are added together and the rider with the lowest number of penalties is the winner. Dressage is always the first element, generally followed by show-jumping and then cross-country. However, if you are eliminated in either of the jumping phases then you are out of the complete competition.

Hunting

This is a winter activity and is a blood sport. Hunt subscribers pay an annual sum (which can be several hundred pounds for some of the prestige hunts) for the pleasure of hunting through the season which lasts from November to March/early April. The subscription depends on the hunt and the numbers of days per week you hunt. Some have waiting lists, so it is not necessarily easy to join.

Whether hunting or draghunting, keep your horse's hindquarters away from hounds so he cannot kick them.

If you know someone who is a member of the local hunt it is possible for them to take you along for a day as a guest. You would probably only be allowed to go for three guest days before you were expected to become a subscriber (assuming there are vacancies).

Hunting has lots of traditions and members of the field are expected to follow certain codes of behaviour. One of the worst sins is overtaking the Master, so do be sure you have brakes on your horse before you go hunting!

Draghunting

This has all the attraction of hunting, ie, the fast rides across country, jumping whatever is in the way, but without having a live animal as the quarry.

Draghunts usually last one to two hours, with the hounds following lines laid by runners. Often the lines take in local cross-country courses, and generally you know where you are going to finish on a draghunt whereas on an ordinary hunt the fox could lead the hounds anywhere.

There are not as many draghunts around the country as there are

Draghunting takes place over set 'lines' or routes which may incorporate hunter trial courses.

On a draghunt, horses and riders can enjoy the thrill of the chase without pursuing a live quarry.

ordinary hunts. Usually the draghunt's subscription is considerably less.

Competition checklist

Rider
Crash hat and silk/velvet cover
Hairnet
Jacket
Shirt and tie/stock & pin
Gloves
Jodhpurs plus overtrousers to wear so jodhs are kept clean until you
    enter the ring
Boots
Spurs (if worn)
Whip as appropriate eg jumping, dressage
Money for entry fees, drinks etc
Packed lunch
Schedule
Dressage test (if applicable)

Horse

Saddle, irons, leathers, girth, numnah, surcingle
Complete bridle
Headcollar and rope
Rugs as appropriate
Travelling bandages and gamgee, hock boots, knee caps
Tail bandage and guard
Protective boots for competition, eg, over-reach boots, brushing boots
Haynet
Feed
Water container and bucket
Grooming kit
First aid kit (including some items for human use as well as equine)
    You may also like to carry spare reins, leathers and girth in case of emergency.

USEFUL ADDRESSES

British Horse Society
British Equestrian Centre
Stoneleigh
Warks, CV8 2LR

British Showjumping Association
(Address as above)

Endurance Horse and Pony Society
Mill House
Mill Lane
Stoke Bruerne
Northants, NN12 7SH

Horse & Pony Magazine
Your Horse Magazine
EMAP
Bretton Court
Bretton
Peterborough, PE3 8DZ

MMB Farmkey
PO Box 42
Southam Road
Banbury
Oxon

Companion to this book

A Guide to Horse Riding
by Lesley Eccles

Now you have your first horse, whether you are happy to remain a weekend rider or seek the thrill of competition, this book provides the ideal introduction for all beginners to horse riding.

- Starting to ride: what to wear, fitness, terminology
- Making progress: the horse's paces, school movements, working without stirrups
- Learning to jump: techniques, show jumping, cross-country riding
- The next stages: examinations, holidays, having a horse on loan

Crowdfunders

Over the autumn of 2019 I ran a crowdfunding campaign to help me meet the costs involved in self-publishing *Banquet of the Beasts*. For sixty days I cajoled, nagged and generally stalked people into advance-buying a book that did not yet exist. Without these people I wouldn't have been able to afford to pay for professional proofreading and editing, and *Banquet of the Beasts* may never have been published.

So a huge heartfelt thanks goes to:

Rahul Agrawal
Sheila Arthur
Marion Back
Gill Becket
Alan Bradford
Hilary Burbank
Sarah Campbell
Therese Christie
Julie Connelly
Katherine Cory
Zhila Faraji
Vicki Fleck

Andrew Flett
Allison Galbraith
Vivien Grahame
Alison Gregory
Gareth Harper
Stephen Hepburn
Alan Hill
Jerry Hutchinson
Matt Jenkinson
Mary Kennedy
Janette Kenyon
Sharron Lea

Priya Logan
Therese Lynch
Fiona Macintosh
Tracey Mcmillan
Jim Morrice
Irina Martin
Louise McVey
Bruce Newlands
Chris Paton
Pamela Payne*
John Richardson
Roxana Romero
Ian Skewis
Soghra Tavasoli

Cameron Taylor
Amanda Thow
Jo Todd
Helen Traill
Martha Wardrop
and Ania Zielinska.

*A particular special mention must go to my mum, Pam. Your more than generous donation to the crowdfunding cause was really appreciated.